PUFFIN B(

Charlie and the Chocolate Factory
James and the Giant Peach
Fantastic Mr Fox

Roald Dahl was born in 1916 in Wales of Norwegian parents. He was educated in England before starting work for the Shell Oil Company in Africa. He began writing after a 'monumental bash on the head' sustained as an RAF fighter pilot during the Second World War. Roald Dahl is one of the most successful and well known of all children's writers. His books, which are read by children the world over, include *James and the Giant Peach*, *Charlie and the Chocolate Factory*, *The Magic Finger*, *Charlie and the Great Glass Elevator*, *Fantastic Mr Fox*, *Matilda*, *The Twits*, *The BFG* and *The Witches*, winner of the 1983 Whitbread Award. Roald Dahl died in 1990 at the age of seventy-four.

Quentin Blake was born in the suburbs of London in 1932. He read English at Cambridge and did a postgraduate certificate in education at London University. From 1949 he worked as a cartoonist for many magazines, most notably *The Spectator* and *Punch*. He moved into children's book illustration, where his inimitable style has won him enormous acclaim. Alongside this he has pursued a teaching career: he was head of the illustration department at the Royal College of Art and is now a visiting Professor. Quentin Blake was awarded the OBE in 1988 and he became the first ever Children's Laureate in 1999.

ROALD DAHL

Charlie and the Chocolate Factory

James and the Giant Peach

Fantastic Mr Fox

Illustrated by
QUENTIN BLAKE

PUFFIN BOOKS

PUFFIN BOOKS

Published by the Penguin Group
Penguin Books Ltd, 27 Wrights Lane, London W8 5TZ, England
Penguin Putnam Inc., 375 Hudson Street, New York, New York 10014, USA
Penguin Books Australia Ltd, Ringwood, Victoria, Australia
Penguin Books Canada Ltd, 10 Alcorn Avenue, Toronto, Ontario, Canada M4V 3B2
Penguin Books India (P) Ltd, 11 Community Centre, Panchsheel Park, New Delhi – 110 017, India
Penguin Books (NZ) Ltd, Cnr Rosedale and Airborne Roads, Albany, Auckland, New Zealand
Penguin Books (South Africa) (Pty) Ltd, 5 Watkins Street, Denver Ext 4, Johannesburg 2094,
South Africa

On the World Wide Web at: www.penguin.com

Penguin Books Ltd, Registered Offices: Harmondsworth, Middlesex, England

Charlie and the Chocolate Factory first published in the USA 1964
Published in Great Britain by George Allen & Unwin 1967
Published in Puffin Books 1973
Reissued with new illustrations 1995
James and the Giant Peach first published in the USA 1961
Published in Great Britain by George Allen & Unwin 1967
Published in Puffin Books 1973
Reissued with new illustrations 1995
Fantastic Mr Fox first published by George Allen & Unwin 1970
Published in Puffin Books 1974
Reissued with new illustrations 1996

This edition published in Puffin Books 2000
2

Text copyright © Roald Dahl Nominee Ltd, 1961, 1964, 1970
Illustrations copyright © Quentin Blake, 1995, 1996
All rights reserved

The moral right of the illustrator has been asserted

Made and printed in Scotland by Omnia Books Ltd.

British Library Cataloguing in Publication Data
A CIP catalogue record for this book is available from the British Library

ISBN 0–141–31163–0

Contents

Charlie
and the
Chocolate Factory

For Theo

Contents

There are five children in this book:

AUGUSTUS GLOOP
A greedy boy

VERUCA SALT
A girl who is spoiled by her parents

VIOLET BEAUREGARDE
A girl who chews gum all day long

MIKE TEAVEE
A boy who does nothing but watch television

and

CHARLIE BUCKET
The hero

I

Here Comes Charlie

These two very old people are the father and
mother of Mr Bucket. Their names are Grandpa
Joe and Grandma Josephine.

And *these* two very old people are the father and mother of Mrs Bucket. Their names are Grandpa George and Grandma Georgina.

This is Mr Bucket. This is Mrs Bucket.
Mr and Mrs Bucket have a small boy whose name is Charlie Bucket.

This is Charlie.

How d'you do? And how d'you do? And how d'you do again? He is pleased to meet you.

The whole of this family – the six grown-ups (count them) and little Charlie Bucket – live together in a small wooden house on the edge of a great town.

The house wasn't nearly large enough for so many people, and life was extremely uncomfortable for them all. There were only two rooms in the place altogether, and there was only one bed. The bed was given to the four old grandparents because they were so old and tired. They were so tired, they never got out of it.

Grandpa Joe and Grandma Josephine on this side, Grandpa George and Grandma Georgina on this side.

Mr and Mrs Bucket and little Charlie Bucket slept in the other room, upon mattresses on the floor.

In the summertime, this wasn't too bad, but in the winter, freezing cold draughts blew across the floor all night long, and it was awful.

There wasn't any question of them being able to buy a better house – or even one more bed to sleep in. They were far too poor for that.

Mr Bucket was the only person in the family with a job. He worked in a toothpaste factory, where he sat all day long at a bench and screwed the little caps on to the tops of the tubes of toothpaste after the tubes had been filled. But a toothpaste cap-screwer is never paid very much money, and poor Mr Bucket, however hard he worked, and however fast he screwed on the caps, was never able to make enough to buy one half of the things that so large a family needed. There wasn't even enough money to buy proper food for them all. The only meals they could afford were bread and margarine for breakfast, boiled potatoes and cabbage for lunch, and cabbage soup for supper. Sundays were a bit better. They all looked forward to Sundays because then, although they had exactly the same, everyone was allowed a second helping.

The Buckets, of course, didn't starve, but every one of them – the two old grandfathers, the two old grandmothers, Charlie's father, Charlie's mother, and especially little Charlie himself – went about from morning till night with a horrible empty feeling in their tummies.

Charlie felt it worst of all. And although his father and mother often went without their own share of lunch or supper so that they could give it to him, it still wasn't nearly enough for a growing boy. He desperately wanted something more filling and satisfying than cabbage and cabbage soup. The one thing he longed for more than anything else was ... CHOCOLATE.

Walking to school in the mornings, Charlie could see great slabs of chocolate piled up high in the shop windows, and he would stop and stare and press his nose against the glass, his mouth watering like mad. Many times a day, he would see other children taking bars of creamy chocolate out of their pockets and munching them greedily, and *that*, of course, was *pure* torture.

Only once a year, on his birthday, did Charlie Bucket ever get to taste a bit of chocolate. The whole family saved up their money for that special occasion, and when the great day arrived, Charlie was always presented with one small chocolate bar to eat all by himself. And each time he received it, on those marvellous birthday mornings, he would place it carefully in a small wooden box that he owned, and treasure it as though it were a bar of solid gold; and for the next few days, he would allow himself only to look at it, but never to touch it. Then at last, when he could stand it no longer, he would peel back a *tiny* bit of the paper wrapping at one corner to expose a *tiny* bit of chocolate, and then he would take a *tiny* nibble – just enough to allow the lovely sweet taste to spread out slowly over his tongue. The next day, he would take another tiny nibble, and so on, and so on. And in this way, Charlie would make his sixpenny bar of birthday chocolate last him for more than a month.

But I haven't yet told you about the one awful thing that tortured little Charlie, the lover of chocolate, more than *anything* else. This thing, for him, was far, far worse than seeing slabs of chocolate in the shop windows or watching other children munching bars of creamy chocolate right in front of him. It was the most terrible torturing thing you could imagine, and it was this:

In the town itself, actually within *sight* of the house in which Charlie lived, there was an ENORMOUS CHOCOLATE FACTORY!

Just imagine that!

And it wasn't simply an ordinary enormous chocolate factory, either. It was the largest and most famous in the whole world! It was WONKA'S FACTORY, owned by a man called Mr Willy Wonka, the greatest inventor and maker of chocolates that there has ever been. And what a tremendous, marvellous place it was! It had huge iron gates leading into it, and a high wall surrounding it, and smoke belching from its chimneys, and strange whizzing sounds coming from deep inside it. And outside the walls, for half a mile around in every direction, the air was scented with the heavy rich smell of melting chocolate!

Twice a day, on his way to and from school, little Charlie Bucket had to walk right past the gates of the factory. And every time he went by, he would begin to walk very, very slowly, and he would hold his nose high in the air and take long deep sniffs of the gorgeous chocolatey smell all around him.

Oh, how he loved that smell!

And oh, how he wished he could go inside the factory and see what it was like!

2

Mr Willy Wonka's Factory

In the evenings, after he had finished his supper of watery cabbage soup, Charlie always went into the room of his four grandparents to listen to their stories, and then afterwards to say good night.

Every one of these old people was over ninety. They were as shrivelled as prunes, and as bony as skeletons, and throughout the day, until Charlie made his appearance, they lay huddled in their one bed, two at either end, with nightcaps on to keep their heads warm, dozing the time away with nothing to do. But as soon as they heard the door opening, and heard Charlie's voice saying, 'Good evening, Grandpa Joe and Grandma Josephine, and Grandpa George and Grandma Georgina,' then all four of them would suddenly sit up, and their old wrinkled faces would light up with smiles of pleasure – and the talking would begin. For they loved this little boy. He was the only bright thing in their lives, and his evening visits were something that they looked forward to all day long. Often, Charlie's mother and father would come in as well, and stand by the door, listening to the stories that the old people told;

and thus, for perhaps half an hour every night, this room would become a happy place, and the whole family would forget that it was hungry and poor.

One evening, when Charlie went in to see his grandparents, he said to them, 'Is it *really* true that Wonka's Chocolate Factory is the biggest in the world?'

'*True?*' cried all four of them at once. 'Of course it's true! Good heavens, didn't you know *that?* It's about *fifty* times as big as any other!'

'And is Mr Willy Wonka *really* the cleverest chocolate maker in the world?'

'My *dear* boy,' said Grandpa Joe, raising himself up a little higher on his pillow, 'Mr Willy Wonka is the most *amazing*, the most *fantastic*, the most *extraordinary* chocolate maker the world has ever seen! I thought *everybody* knew that!'

'I knew he was famous, Grandpa Joe, and I knew he was very clever . . .'

'*Clever!*' cried the old man. 'He's more than that! He's a *magician* with chocolate! He can make *anything* – anything he wants! Isn't that a fact, my dears?'

The other three old people nodded their heads slowly up and down, and said, '*Absolutely* true. *Just* as true as can be.'

And Grandpa Joe said, 'You mean to say I've never *told* you about Mr Willy Wonka and his factory?'

'Never,' answered little Charlie.

'Good heavens above! I don't know what's the matter with me!'

'Will you tell me now, Grandpa Joe, please?'

'I certainly will. Sit down beside me on the bed, my dear, and listen carefully.'

Grandpa Joe was the oldest of the four grandparents. He was ninety-six and a half, and that is just about as old as anybody can be. Like all extremely old people, he was delicate and weak, and throughout the day he spoke very little. But in the evenings, when Charlie, his beloved grandson, was in the room, he seemed in some marvellous way to grow quite young again. All his tiredness fell away from him, and he became as eager and excited as a young boy.

'Oh, what a man he is, this Mr Willy Wonka!' cried Grandpa Joe. 'Did you know, for example, that he has himself invented more than two hundred new kinds of chocolate bars, each with a different centre, each far sweeter and creamier and more delicious than anything the other chocolate factories can make!'

'Perfectly true!' cried Grandma Josephine. 'And he sends them to *all* the four corners of the earth! Isn't that so, Grandpa Joe?'

'It is, my dear, it is. And to all the kings and presidents of the world as well. But it isn't only chocolate bars that he makes. Oh, dear me, no! He has some really *fantastic* inventions up his sleeve, Mr Willy Wonka has! Did you know that he's invented a way of making chocolate ice cream so that it stays cold for hours and hours without being in the refrigerator? You can even leave it lying in the sun all morning on a hot day and it won't go runny!'

'But that's *impossible*!' said little Charlie, staring at his grandfather.

'Of course it's impossible!' cried Grandpa Joe. 'It's completely *absurd*! But Mr Willy Wonka has done it!'

'Quite right!' the others agreed, nodding their heads. 'Mr Wonka has done it.'

'And then again,' Grandpa Joe went on speaking very slowly now so that Charlie wouldn't miss a word, 'Mr Willy Wonka can make marshmallows that taste of violets, and rich caramels that change colour every ten seconds as you suck them, and little feathery sweets that melt away deliciously the moment you put them between your lips. He can make chewing-gum that never loses its taste, and sugar balloons that you can blow up to enormous sizes before you pop them with a pin and gobble them up. And, by a most secret method, he can make lovely blue birds' eggs with black spots on them, and when you put one of these in your mouth, it gradually gets smaller and smaller until suddenly there is nothing left except a tiny little pink sugary baby bird sitting on the tip of your tongue.'

Grandpa Joe paused and ran the point of his tongue slowly over his lips. 'It makes my mouth water just *thinking* about it,' he said.

'Mine, too,' said little Charlie. 'But *please* go on.'

While they were talking, Mr and Mrs Bucket, Charlie's mother and father, had come quietly into the room, and now both were standing just inside the door, listening.

'Tell Charlie about that crazy Indian prince,' said Grandma Josephine. 'He'd like to hear that.'

'You mean Prince Pondicherry?' said Grandpa Joe, and he began chuckling with laughter.

'*Completely* dotty!' said Grandpa George.

'But *very* rich,' said Grandma Georgina.

'What did he do?' asked Charlie eagerly.

'Listen,' said Grandpa Joe, 'and I'll tell you.'

3

Mr Wonka and the Indian Prince

'Prince Pondicherry wrote a letter to Mr Willy Wonka,' said Grandpa Joe, 'and asked him to come all the way out to India and build him a colossal palace entirely out of chocolate.'

'Did Mr Wonka do it, Grandpa?'

'He did, indeed. And what a palace it was! It had one hundred rooms, and *everything* was made of either dark or light chocolate! The bricks were chocolate, and the cement holding them together was chocolate, and the windows were chocolate, and all the walls and ceilings were made of chocolate, so were the carpets and the pictures and the furniture and the beds; and when you turned on the taps in the bathroom, hot chocolate came pouring out.

'When it was all finished, Mr Wonka said to Prince Pondicherry, "I warn you, though, it won't last very long, so you'd better start eating it right away."

'"Nonsense!" shouted the Prince. "I'm not going to eat my palace! I'm not even going to nibble the staircase or lick the walls! I'm going to *live* in it!"

'But Mr Wonka was right, of course, because

23

soon after this, there came a very hot day with a boiling sun, and the whole palace began to melt, and then it sank slowly to the ground, and the crazy prince, who was dozing in the living room at the time, woke up to find himself swimming around in a huge brown sticky lake of chocolate.'

Little Charlie sat very still on the edge of the bed, staring at his grandfather. Charlie's face was bright, and his eyes were stretched so wide you could see the whites all around. 'Is all this *really* true?' he asked. 'Or are you pulling my leg?'

'It's true!' cried all four of the old people at once. 'Of course it's true! Ask anyone you like!'

'And I'll tell you something else that's true,' said Grandpa Joe, and now he leaned closer to Charlie, and lowered his voice to a soft, secret whisper. '*Nobody . . . ever . . . comes . . . out!*'

'Out of where?' asked Charlie.

'*And . . . nobody . . . ever . . . goes . . . in!*'

'In *where*?' cried Charlie.

'Wonka's factory, of course!'

'Grandpa, what *do* you mean?'

'I mean *workers*, Charlie.'

'Workers?'

'All factories,' said Grandpa Joe, 'have workers streaming in and out of the gates in the mornings and evenings – except Wonka's! Have *you* ever seen a single person going into that place – or coming out?'

Little Charlie looked slowly around at each of the four old faces, one after the other, and they all looked back at him. They were friendly smiling faces, but they were also quite serious. There was no sign of joking or leg-pulling on any of them.

'Well? Have *you*?' asked Grandpa Joe.

'I . . . I really don't know, Grandpa,' Charlie stammered. 'Whenever I walk past the factory, the gates seem to be closed.'

'Exactly!' said Grandpa Joe.

'But there *must* be people working there . . . '

'Not *people*, Charlie. Not *ordinary* people, anyway.'

'Then who?' cried Charlie.

'Ah-ha . . . That's it, you see . . . That's another of Mr Willy Wonka's clevernesses.'

'Charlie, dear,' Mrs Bucket called out from where she was standing by the door, 'it's time for bed. That's enough for tonight.'

'But, Mother, I *must* hear . . . '

'Tomorrow, my darling . . . '

'That's right,' said Grandpa Joe, 'I'll tell you the rest of it tomorrow evening.'

4

The Secret Workers

The next evening, Grandpa Joe went on with his story.

'You see, Charlie,' he said, 'not so very long ago there used to be thousands of people working in Mr Willy Wonka's factory. Then one day, all of a sudden, Mr Wonka had to ask *every single one of them* to leave, to go home, never to come back.'

'But why?' asked Charlie.

'Because of spies.'

'Spies?'

'Yes. All the other chocolate makers, you see, had begun to grow jealous of the wonderful sweets that Mr Wonka was making, and they started sending in spies to steal his secret recipes. The spies took jobs in the Wonka factory, pretending that they were ordinary workers, and while they were there, each one of them found out exactly how a certain special thing was made.'

'And did they go back to their own factories and tell?' asked Charlie.

'They must have,' answered Grandpa Joe, 'because soon after that, Fickelgruber's factory started making an ice cream that would never melt, even in the hottest sun. Then Mr Prodnose's factory came out with a chewing-gum that never lost its flavour however much you chewed it. And then Mr Slugworth's factory began making sugar balloons that you could blow up to huge sizes before you popped them with a pin and gobbled them up. And so on, and so on. And Mr Willy Wonka tore his beard and shouted, "This is terrible! I shall be ruined! There are spies everywhere! I shall have to close the factory!"'

'But he didn't do that!' Charlie said.

'Oh, yes he did. He told *all* the workers that he was sorry, but they would have to go home. Then, he shut the main gates and fastened them with a chain. And suddenly, Wonka's giant chocolate factory became silent and deserted. The chimneys stopped smoking, the machines stopped whirring, and from then on, not a single chocolate or sweet was made. Not a soul went in or out, and even Mr Willy Wonka himself disappeared completely.

'Months and months went by,' Grandpa Joe

went on, 'but still the factory remained closed. And everybody said, "Poor Mr Wonka. He was so nice. And he made such marvellous things. But he's finished now. It's all over."

'Then something astonishing happened. One day, early in the morning, thin columns of white smoke were seen to be coming out of the tops of the tall chimneys of the factory! People in the town stopped and stared. "What's going on?" they cried. "Someone's lit the furnaces! Mr Wonka must be opening up again!" They ran to the gates, expecting to see them wide open and Mr Wonka standing there to welcome his workers back.

'But no! The great iron gates were still locked and chained as securely as ever, and Mr Wonka was nowhere to be seen.

'"But the factory *is* working!" the people shouted. "Listen! You can hear the machines! They're all whirring again! And you can smell the smell of melting chocolate in the air!"'

Grandpa Joe leaned forward and laid a long bony finger on Charlie's knee, and he said softly, 'But most mysterious of all, Charlie, were the shadows in the windows of the factory. The people standing on the street outside could see small dark shadows moving about behind the frosted glass windows.'

'Shadows of whom?' said Charlie quickly.

'That's exactly what everybody else wanted to know.

'"The place is full of workers!" the people shouted. "But nobody's gone in! The gates are locked! It's crazy! Nobody ever comes out, either!"

'But there was no question at all,' said Grandpa Joe, 'that the factory was running. And it's gone on running ever since, for these last ten years. What's more, the chocolates and sweets it's been turning out have become more fantastic and delicious all the time. And of course now when Mr Wonka invents some new and wonderful sweet, neither Mr Fickelgruber nor Mr Prodnose nor Mr Slugworth nor anybody else is able to copy it. No spies can go into the factory to find out how it is made.'

'But Grandpa, *who*,' cried Charlie, '*who* is Mr Wonka using to do all the work in the factory?'

'Nobody knows, Charlie.'

'But that's *absurd*! Hasn't someone asked Mr Wonka?'

'Nobody sees him any more. He never comes out. The only things that come out of that place are chocolates and sweets. They come out through a special trap door in the wall, all packed and addressed, and they are picked up every day by Post Office trucks.'

'But Grandpa, what *sort* of people are they that work in there?'

'My dear boy,' said Grandpa Joe, 'that is one of the great mysteries of the chocolate-making world. We know only one thing about them. They are very small. The faint shadows that sometimes appear behind the windows, especially late at night when the lights are on, are those of *tiny* people, people no taller than my knee . . . '

'There aren't any such people,' Charlie said.

Just then, Mr Bucket, Charlie's father, came into the room. He was home from the toothpaste factory, and he was waving an evening newspaper rather excitedly. 'Have you heard the news?' he cried. He held up the paper so that they could see the huge headline. The headline said:

WONKA FACTORY TO BE OPENED AT LAST TO LUCKY FEW

5

The Golden Tickets

'You mean people are actually going to be allowed
to go inside the factory?' cried Grandpa Joe. 'Read
us what it says – quickly!'

'All right,' said Mr Bucket, smoothing out the
newspaper. 'Listen.'

Evening Bulletin

*Mr Willy Wonka, the confectionery genius
whom nobody has seen for the last ten years,
sent out the following notice today:*

**I, Willy Wonka, have decided to allow five
children – just *five*, mind you, and no more – to
visit my factory this year. These lucky five will
be shown around personally by me, and they
will be allowed to see all the secrets and the
magic of my factory. Then, at the end of the
tour, as a special present, all of them will be
given enough chocolates and sweets to last them
for the rest of their lives! So watch out for the
Golden Tickets! Five Golden Tickets have been**

printed on golden paper, and these five Golden Tickets have been hidden underneath the ordinary wrapping paper of five ordinary bars of chocolate. These five chocolate bars may be anywhere – in any shop in any street in any town in any country in the world – upon any counter where Wonka's Sweets are sold. And the five lucky finders of these five Golden Tickets are the *only* ones who will be allowed to visit my factory and see what it's like *now* inside! Good luck to you all, and happy hunting! (Signed Willy Wonka.)

'The man's dotty!' muttered Grandma Josephine.

'He's brilliant!' cried Grandpa Joe. 'He's a magician! Just imagine what will happen now! The whole world will be searching for those Golden Tickets! Everyone will be buying Wonka's chocolate bars in the hope of finding one! He'll sell more than ever before! Oh, how exciting it would be to find one!'

'And all the chocolate and sweets that you could eat for the rest of your life – *free*!' said Grandpa George. 'Just imagine that!'

'They'd have to deliver them in a truck!' said Grandma Georgina.

'It makes me quite ill to think of it,' said Grandma Josephine.

'Nonsense!' cried Grandpa Joe. 'Wouldn't it be *something*, Charlie, to open a bar of chocolate and see a Golden Ticket glistening inside!'

'It certainly would, Grandpa. But there isn't a hope,' Charlie said sadly. 'I only get one bar a year.'

'You never know, darling,' said Grandma Georgina. 'It's your birthday next week. You have as much chance as anybody else.'

'I'm afraid that simply isn't true,' said Grandpa George. 'The kids who are going to find the Golden Tickets are the ones who can afford to buy bars of chocolate every day. Our Charlie gets only one a year. There isn't a hope.'

6

The First Two Finders

The very next day, the first Golden Ticket was found. The finder was a boy called Augustus Gloop, and Mr Bucket's evening newspaper carried a large picture of him on the front page. The picture showed a nine-year-old boy who was so enormously fat he looked as though he had been blown up with a powerful pump. Great flabby folds of fat bulged out from every part of his body, and his face was like a monstrous ball of dough with two small greedy curranty eyes peering out upon the world. The town in which Augustus Gloop lived, the newspaper said, had gone wild with excitement over their hero. Flags were flying from all the windows, children had been given a holiday from school, and a parade was being organized in honour of the famous youth.

'I just *knew* Augustus would find a Golden Ticket,' his mother had told the newspapermen. 'He eats *so many* bars of chocolate a day that it was almost *impossible* for him *not* to find one. Eating is his hobby, you know. That's *all* he's interested in. But still, that's better than being a *hooligan* and shooting off *zip guns* and things like that in his

spare time, isn't it? And what I always say is, he
wouldn't go on eating like he does unless he *needed*
nourishment, would he? It's all *vitamins*, anyway.
What a *thrill* it will be for him to visit Mr Wonka's
marvellous factory! We're just as *proud* as
anything!'

'What a revolting woman,' said Grandma
Josephine.

'And what a repulsive boy,' said Grandma Georgina.

'Only four Golden Tickets left,' said Grandpa George. 'I wonder who'll get *those*.'

And now the whole country, indeed, the whole world, seemed suddenly to be caught up in a mad chocolate-buying spree, everybody searching frantically for those precious remaining tickets. Fully grown women were seen going into sweet shops and buying ten Wonka bars at a time, then tearing off the wrappers on the spot and peering eagerly underneath for a glint of golden paper. Children were taking hammers and smashing their piggy banks and running out to the shops with handfuls of money. In one city, a famous gangster robbed a bank of a thousand pounds and spent the whole lot on Wonka bars that same afternoon. And when the police entered his house to arrest him, they found him sitting on the floor amidst mountains of chocolate, ripping off the wrappers with the blade of a long dagger. In far-off Russia, a woman called Charlotte Russe claimed to have found the second ticket, but it turned out to be a clever fake. The famous English scientist, Professor Foulbody, invented a machine which would tell you at once, without opening the wrapper of a bar of chocolate, whether or not there was a Golden Ticket hidden underneath it. The machine had a mechanical arm that shot out with tremendous force and grabbed hold of anything that had the slightest bit of gold inside it, and for a moment, it looked like the answer to everything. But unfortunately, while the

Professor was showing off the machine to the public at the sweet counter of a large department store, the mechanical arm shot out and made a grab for the gold filling in the back tooth of a duchess who was standing near by. There was an ugly scene, and the machine was smashed by the crowd.

Suddenly, on the day before Charlie Bucket's birthday, the newspapers announced that the second Golden Ticket had been found. The lucky person was a small girl called Veruca Salt who lived with her rich parents in a great city far away. Once again Mr Bucket's evening newspaper carried

a big picture of the finder. She was sitting between her beaming father and mother in the living room of their house, waving the Golden Ticket above her head, and grinning from ear to ear.

Veruca's father, Mr Salt, had eagerly explained to the newspapermen exactly how the ticket was found. 'You see, boys,' he had said, 'as soon as my little girl told me that she simply *had* to have one of those Golden Tickets, I went out into the town and started buying up all the Wonka bars I could lay my hands on. *Thousands* of them, I must have bought. *Hundreds* of thousands! Then I had them loaded on to trucks and sent directly to my own factory. I'm in the peanut business, you see, and I've got about a hundred women working for me over at my place, shelling peanuts for roasting and salting. That's what they do all day long, those women, they sit there shelling peanuts. So I says to them, "Okay, girls," I says, "from now on, you can stop shelling peanuts and start shelling the wrappers off these chocolate bars instead!" And they did. I had every worker in the place yanking the paper off those bars of chocolate full speed ahead from morning till night.

'But three days went by, and we had no luck. Oh, it was terrible! My little Veruca got more and more upset each day, and every time I went home she would scream at me, "*Where's my Golden Ticket! I want my Golden Ticket!*" And she would lie for hours on the floor, kicking and yelling in the most disturbing way. Well, I just hated to see my little girl feeling unhappy like that, so I vowed I would keep up the search until I'd got her what she wanted. Then suddenly . . . on the evening of the fourth day, one of my women workers yelled, "I've got it! A Golden Ticket!" And I said, "Give it to me, quick!" and she did, and I rushed it home and gave it to my darling Veruca, and now she's all smiles, and we have a happy home once again.'

'That's even worse than the fat boy,' said Grandma Josephine.

'She needs a really good spanking,' said Grandma Georgina.

'I don't think the girl's father played it quite fair, Grandpa, do you?' Charlie murmured.

'He spoils her,' Grandpa Joe said. 'And no good can ever come from spoiling a child like that, Charlie, you mark my words.'

'Come to bed, my darling,' said Charlie's mother. 'Tomorrow's your birthday, don't forget that, so I expect you'll be up early to open your present.'

'A Wonka chocolate bar!' cried Charlie. 'It is a Wonka bar, isn't it?'

'Yes, my love,' his mother said. 'Of course it is.'

'Oh, wouldn't it be wonderful if I found the third Golden Ticket inside it?' Charlie said.

'Bring it in here when you get it,' Grandpa Joe said. 'Then we can all watch you taking off the wrapper.'

7

Charlie's Birthday

'Happy birthday!' cried the four old grandparents, as Charlie came into their room early the next morning.

Charlie smiled nervously and sat down on the edge of the bed. He was holding his present, his only present, very carefully in his two hands. WONKA'S WHIPPLE-SCRUMPTIOUS FUDGEMALLOW DELIGHT, it said on the wrapper.

The four old people, two at either end of the bed, propped themselves up on their pillows and stared with anxious eyes at the bar of chocolate in Charlie's hands.

Mr and Mrs Bucket came in and stood at the foot of the bed, watching Charlie.

The room became silent. Everybody was waiting now for Charlie to start opening his present. Charlie looked down at the bar of chocolate. He ran his fingers slowly back and forth along the length of it, stroking it lovingly, and the shiny paper wrapper made little sharp crackly noises in the quiet room.

Then Mrs Bucket said gently, 'You mustn't be too disappointed, my darling, if you don't find what you're looking for underneath that wrapper. You really can't expect to be as lucky as all that.'

'She's quite right,' Mr Bucket said.

Charlie didn't say anything.

'After all,' Grandma Josephine said, 'in the whole wide world there are only three tickets left to be found.'

'The thing to remember,' Grandma Georgina said, 'is that whatever happens, you'll still have the bar of chocolate.'

'Wonka's Whipple-Scrumptious Fudgemallow Delight!' cried Grandpa George. 'It's the best of them all! You'll just *love* it!'

'Yes,' Charlie whispered. 'I know.'

'Just forget all about those Golden Tickets and enjoy the chocolate,' Grandpa Joe said. 'Why don't you do that?'

They all knew it was ridiculous to expect this one poor little bar of chocolate to have a magic ticket inside it, and they were trying as gently and as kindly as they could to prepare Charlie for the disappointment. But there was one other thing that the grown-ups also knew, and it was this: that however *small* the chance might be of striking lucky, *the chance was there*.

The chance *had* to be there.

This particular bar of chocolate had as much chance as any other of having a Golden Ticket.

And that was why all the grandparents and parents in the room were actually just as tense and excited as Charlie was, although they were pretending to be very calm.

'You'd better go ahead and open it up, or you'll be late for school,' Grandpa Joe said.

'You might as well get it over with,' Grandpa George said.

'Open it, my dear,' Grandma Georgina said. 'Please open it. You're making me jumpy.'

Very slowly, Charlie's fingers began to tear open one small corner of the wrapping paper.

The old people in the bed all leaned forward, craning their scraggy necks.

Then suddenly, as though he couldn't bear the suspense any longer, Charlie tore the wrapper right down the middle . . . and on to his lap, there fell . . . a light-brown creamy-coloured bar of chocolate.

There was no sign of a Golden Ticket anywhere.

'Well – that's *that*!' said Grandpa Joe brightly. 'It's just what we expected.'

Charlie looked up. Four kind old faces were watching him intently from the bed. He smiled at them, a small sad smile, and then he shrugged his shoulders and picked up the chocolate bar and held it out to his mother, and said, 'Here, Mother, have a bit. We'll share it. I want everybody to taste it.'

'Certainly not!' his mother said.

And the others all cried, 'No, no! We wouldn't dream of it! It's *all* yours!'

'*Please*,' begged Charlie, turning round and offering it to Grandpa Joe.

But neither he nor anyone else would take even a tiny bit.

'It's time to go to school, my darling,' Mrs Bucket said, putting an arm around Charlie's skinny shoulders. 'Come on, or you'll be late.'

8

Two More Golden Tickets Found

That evening, Mr Bucket's newspaper announced the finding of not only the third Golden Ticket, but the fourth as well. TWO GOLDEN TICKETS FOUND TODAY, screamed the headlines. ONLY ONE MORE LEFT.

'All right,' said Grandpa Joe, when the whole family was gathered in the old people's room after supper, 'let's hear who found them.'

'The third ticket,' read Mr Bucket, holding the newspaper up close to his face because his eyes were bad and he couldn't afford glasses, 'the third ticket was found by a Miss Violet Beauregarde. There was great excitement in the Beauregarde household when our reporter arrived to interview the lucky young lady – cameras were clicking and flashbulbs were flashing and people were pushing and jostling and trying to get a bit closer to the famous girl. And the famous girl was standing on a chair in the living room waving the Golden Ticket madly at arm's length as though she were flagging a taxi. She was talking very fast and very loudly to everyone, but it was not easy to hear all that she

said because she was chewing so ferociously upon a piece of gum at the same time.

'"I'm a gum chewer, normally," she shouted, "but when I heard about these ticket things of Mr Wonka's, I gave up gum and started on chocolate bars in the hope of striking lucky. *Now*, of course, I'm back on gum. I just *adore* gum. I can't do without it. I munch it all day long except for a few minutes at mealtimes when I take it out and stick it behind my ear for safekeeping. To tell you the truth, I simply wouldn't feel *comfortable* if I didn't have that little wedge of gum to chew on every moment of the day, I really wouldn't. My mother says it's not ladylike and it looks ugly to see a girl's jaws going up and down like mine do all the time, but I don't agree. And who's she to criticize, anyway, because if you ask me, I'd say that *her* jaws are going up and down almost as much as mine are just from *yelling* at me every minute of the day."

'"Now, Violet," Mrs Beauregarde said from a far corner of the room where she was standing on the piano to avoid being trampled by the mob.

'"All right, Mother, keep your hair on!" Miss Beauregarde shouted. "And now," she went on, turning to the reporters again, "it may interest you to know that this piece of gum I'm chewing right at this moment is one I've been working on for over *three months solid*. That's a record, that is. It's beaten the record held by my best friend, Miss Cornelia Prinzmetel. And was she furious! It's my most treasured possession now, this piece of gum is. At night-time, I just stick it on the end of the bedpost, and it's as good as ever in the mornings – a bit hard at first, maybe, but it soon softens up again after I've given it a few good chews. Before I started chewing for the world record, I used to change my piece of gum once a day. I used to do it in our lift on the way home from school. Why the lift? Because I liked sticking the gooey piece that I'd just finished with on to one of the control buttons. Then the next person who came along and pressed the button got my old gum on the end of his or her finger. Ha-ha! And what a racket they kicked up, some of them. You get the best results

46

with women who have expensive gloves on. Oh yes, I'm thrilled to be going to Mr Wonka's factory. And I understand that afterwards he's going to give me enough gum to last me for the rest of my whole life. Whoopee! Hooray!"'

'*Beastly* girl,' said Grandma Josephine.

'Despicable!' said Grandma Georgina. 'She'll come to a sticky end one day, chewing all that gum, you see if she doesn't.'

'And who got the fourth Golden Ticket?' Charlie asked.

'Now, let me see,' said Mr Bucket, peering at the newspaper again. 'Ah yes, here we are. The fourth Golden Ticket,' he read, 'was found by a boy called Mike Teavee.'

'Another bad lot, I'll be bound,' muttered Grandma Josephine.

'Don't interrupt, Grandma,' said Mrs Bucket.

'The Teavee household,' said Mr Bucket, going on with his reading, 'was crammed, like all the others, with excited visitors when our reporter arrived, but young Mike Teavee, the lucky winner, seemed extremely annoyed by the whole business. "Can't you fools see I'm watching television?" he said angrily. "I wish you wouldn't interrupt!"

'The nine-year-old boy was seated before an enormous television set, with his eyes glued to the screen, and he was watching a film in which one bunch of gangsters was shooting up another bunch of gangsters with machine guns. Mike Teavee himself had no less than eighteen toy pistols of various sizes hanging from belts around his body, and

every now and again he would leap up into the air and fire off half a dozen rounds from one or another of these weapons.

'"Quiet!" he shouted, when someone tried to ask him a question. "Didn't I *tell* you not to interrupt! This show's an absolute whiz-banger! It's terrific! I watch it every day. I watch all of them every day, even the rotten ones, where there's no shooting. I like the gangsters best. They're terrific, those gangsters! Especially when they start pumping each other full of lead, or flashing the old stilettos, or giving each other the one-two-three with their knuckledusters! Gosh, what wouldn't I give to be doing that myself! It's the *life*, I tell you! It's terrific!"'

'That's quite enough!' snapped Grandma Josephine. 'I can't *bear* to listen to it!'

'Nor me,' said Grandma Georgina. 'Do *all* children behave like this nowadays – like these brats we've been hearing about?'

'Of course not,' said Mr Bucket, smiling at the old lady in the bed. 'Some do, of course. In fact, quite a lot of them do. But not *all*.'

'And now there's only *one ticket left*!' said Grandpa George.

'Quite so,' sniffed Grandma Georgina. 'And just as sure as I'll be having cabbage soup for supper tomorrow, that ticket'll go to some nasty little beast who doesn't deserve it!'

9

Grandpa Joe Takes a Gamble

The next day, when Charlie came home from school and went in to see his grandparents, he found that only Grandpa Joe was awake. The other three were all snoring loudly.

'Ssshh!' whispered Grandpa Joe, and he beckoned Charlie to come closer. Charlie tiptoed over and stood beside the bed. The old man gave Charlie a sly grin, and then he started rummaging under his pillow with one hand; and when the hand came out again, there was an ancient leather purse clutched in the fingers. Under cover of the bedclothes, the old man opened the purse and tipped it upside down. Out fell a single silver sixpence. 'It's my secret hoard,' he whispered. 'The others don't know I've got it. And now, you and I are going to have one more fling at finding that last ticket. How about it, eh? But you'll have to help me.'

'Are you *sure* you want to spend your money on that, Grandpa?' Charlie whispered.

'Of course I'm sure!' spluttered the old man excitedly. 'Don't stand there arguing! I'm as keen as you are to find that ticket! Here – take the money and run down the street to the nearest shop and buy the first Wonka bar you see and bring it straight back to me, and we'll open it together.'

Charlie took the little silver coin, and slipped quickly out of the room. In five minutes, he was back.

'Have you got it?' whispered Grandpa Joe, his eyes shining with excitement.

Charlie nodded and held out the bar of chocolate. WONKA'S NUTTY CRUNCH SUR-PRISE, it said on the wrapper.

'Good!' the old man whispered, sitting up in the bed and rubbing his hands. 'Now – come over here and sit close to me and we'll open it together. Are you ready?'

'Yes,' Charlie said. 'I'm ready.'

'All right. You tear off the first bit.'

'No,' Charlie said, 'you paid for it. You do it all.'

The old man's fingers were trembling most ter-ribly as they fumbled with the wrapper. 'We don't have a hope, really,' he whispered, giggling a bit. 'You do know we don't have a hope, don't you?'

'Yes,' Charlie said. 'I know that.'

They looked at each other, and both started giggling nervously.

'Mind you,' said Grandpa Joe, 'there is just that *tiny* chance that it *might* be the one, don't you agree?'

'Yes,' Charlie said. 'Of course. Why don't you open it, Grandpa?'

'All in good time, my boy, all in good time. Which end do you think I ought to open first?'

51

'That corner. The one furthest from you. Just tear off a *tiny* bit, but not quite enough for us to see anything.'

'Like that?' said the old man.

'Yes. Now a little bit more.'

'You finish it,' said Grandpa Joe. 'I'm too nervous.'

'No, Grandpa. You must do it yourself.'

'Very well, then. Here goes.' He tore off the wrapper.

They both stared at what lay underneath. It was a bar of chocolate – nothing more.

All at once, they both saw the funny side of the whole thing, and they burst into peals of laughter.

'What on earth's going on!' cried Grandma Josephine, waking up suddenly.

'Nothing,' said Grandpa Joe. 'You go on back to sleep.'

The Family Begins to Starve

During the next two weeks, the weather turned very cold. First came the snow. It began very suddenly one morning just as Charlie Bucket was getting dressed for school. Standing by the window, he saw the huge flakes drifting slowly down out of an icy sky that was the colour of steel.

By evening, it lay four feet deep around the tiny house, and Mr Bucket had to dig a path from the front door to the road.

After the snow, there came a freezing gale that blew for days and days without stopping. And oh, how bitter cold it was! Everything that Charlie touched seemed to be made of ice, and each time he stepped outside the door, the wind was like a knife on his cheek.

Inside the house, little jets of freezing air came rushing in through the sides of the windows and under the doors, and there was no place to go to escape them. The four old ones lay silent and huddled in their bed, trying to keep the cold out of their bones. The excitement over the Golden Tickets had long since been forgotten. Nobody in the family gave a thought now to anything except the two vital problems of trying to keep warm and trying to get enough to eat.

There is something about very cold weather that gives one an enormous appetite. Most of us find ourselves beginning to crave rich steaming stews and hot apple pies and all kinds of delicious warming dishes; and because we are all a great deal luckier than we realize, we usually get what we want – or near enough. But Charlie Bucket never got what he wanted because the family couldn't afford it, and as the cold weather went on and on, he became ravenously and desperately hungry. Both bars of chocolate, the birthday one and the one Grandpa Joe had bought, had long since been nibbled away, and all he got now were those thin, cabbagy meals three times a day.

Then all at once, the meals became even thinner.

The reason for this was that the toothpaste factory, the place where Mr Bucket worked, suddenly went bust and had to close down. Quickly, Mr Bucket tried to get another job. But he had no luck. In the end, the only way in which he managed to earn a few pennies was by shovelling snow in the streets. But it wasn't enough to buy even a quarter of the food that seven people needed. The situation became desperate. Breakfast was a single slice of bread for each person now, and lunch was maybe half a boiled potato.

Slowly but surely, everybody in the house began to starve.

And every day, little Charlie Bucket, trudging

through the snow on his way to school, would have to pass Mr Willy Wonka's giant chocolate factory. And every day, as he came near to it, he would lift his small pointed nose high in the air and sniff the wonderful sweet smell of melting chocolate. Sometimes, he would stand motionless outside the gates for several minutes on end, taking deep swallowing breaths as though he were trying to *eat* the smell itself.

'That child,' said Grandpa Joe, poking his head up from under the blanket one icy morning, 'that child has *got* to have more food. It doesn't matter about us. We're too old to bother with. But a *growing boy*! He can't go on like this! He's beginning to look like a skeleton!'

'What can one *do*?' murmured Grandma Josephine miserably. 'He refuses to take any of ours. I hear his mother tried to slip her own piece of bread on to his plate at breakfast this morning, but he wouldn't touch it. He made her take it back.'

'He's a fine little fellow,' said Grandpa George. 'He deserves better than this.'

The cruel weather went on and on.

And every day, Charlie Bucket grew thinner and thinner. His face became frighteningly white and pinched. The skin was drawn so tightly over the cheeks that you could see the shapes of the bones underneath. It seemed doubtful whether he could go on much longer like this without becoming dangerously ill.

And now, very calmly, with that curious wisdom

that seems to come so often to small children in times of hardship, he began to make little changes here and there in some of the things that he did, so as to save his strength. In the mornings, he left the house ten minutes earlier so that he could walk slowly to school, without ever having to run. He sat quietly in the classroom during break, resting himself, while the others rushed outdoors and threw snowballs and wrestled in the snow. Everything he did now, he did slowly and carefully, to prevent exhaustion.

Then one afternoon, walking back home with the icy wind in his face (and incidentally feeling hungrier than he had ever felt before), his eye was caught suddenly by something silvery lying in the gutter, in the snow. Charlie stepped off the kerb and bent down to examine it. Part of it was buried under the snow, but he saw at once what it was.

It was a fifty-pence piece!

Quickly he looked around him.

Had somebody just dropped it?

No – that was impossible because of the way part of it was buried.

Several people went hurrying past him on the pavement, their chins sunk deep in the collars of their coats, their feet crunching in the snow. None of them was searching for any money; none of them was taking the slightest notice of the small boy crouching in the gutter.

Then was it *his,* this fifty pence?

Could he *have* it?

Carefully, Charlie pulled it out from under the

snow. It was damp and dirty, but otherwise perfect.

A WHOLE fifty pence!

He held it tightly between his shivering fingers, gazing down at it. It meant one thing to him at that moment, only *one* thing. It meant FOOD.

Automatically, Charlie turned and began moving towards the nearest shop. It was only ten paces away . . . it was a newspaper and stationery shop, the kind that sells almost everything, including sweets and cigars . . . and what he would *do*, he whispered quickly to himself . . . he would buy one luscious bar of chocolate and eat it *all* up, every bit of it, right then and there . . . and the rest of the money he would take straight back home and give to his mother.

The Miracle

Charlie entered the shop and laid the damp fifty pence on the counter.

'One Wonka's Whipple-Scrumptious Fudge-mallow Delight,' he said, remembering how much he had loved the one he had on his birthday.

The man behind the counter looked fat and well-fed. He had big lips and fat cheeks and a very fat neck. The fat around his neck bulged out all around the top of his collar like a rubber ring. He turned and reached behind him for the chocolate bar, then he turned back again and handed it to Charlie. Charlie grabbed it and quickly tore off the wrapper and took an enormous bite. Then he took another ... and another ... and oh, the joy of being able to cram large pieces of something sweet and solid into one's mouth! The sheer blissful joy of being able to fill one's mouth with rich solid food!

'You look like you wanted that one, sonny,' the shopkeeper said pleasantly.

Charlie nodded, his mouth bulging with chocolate.

The shopkeeper put Charlie's change on the counter. 'Take it easy,' he said. 'It'll give you a tummy-ache if you swallow it like that without chewing.'

Charlie went on wolfing the chocolate. He couldn't stop. And in less than half a minute, the whole thing had disappeared down his throat. He was quite out of breath, but he felt marvellously, extraordinarily happy. He reached out a hand to take the change. Then he paused. His eyes were just above the level of the counter. They were staring at the silver coins lying there. The coins were all five-penny pieces. There were nine of them altogether. Surely it wouldn't matter if he spent just one more . . .

'I think,' he said quietly, 'I think . . . I'll have just one more of those chocolate bars. The same kind as before, please.'

'Why not?' the fat shopkeeper said, reaching behind him again and taking another Whipple-

Scrumptious Fudgemallow Delight from the shelf. He laid it on the counter.

Charlie picked it up and tore off the wrapper . . . and *suddenly* . . . from underneath the wrapper . . . there came a brilliant flash of gold.

Charlie's heart stood still.

'It's a Golden Ticket!' screamed the shopkeeper, leaping about a foot in the air. 'You've got a Golden Ticket! You've found the last Golden Ticket! Hey, would you believe it! Come and look at this, everybody! The kid's found Wonka's last Golden Ticket! There it is! It's right here in his hands!'

It seemed as though the shopkeeper might be going to have a fit. 'In my shop, too!' he yelled. 'He found it right here in my own little shop! Somebody call the newspapers quick and let them know! Watch out now, sonny! Don't tear it as you unwrap it! That thing's precious!'

In a few seconds, there was a crowd of about twenty people clustering around Charlie, and many more were pushing their way in from the street. Everybody wanted to get a look at the Golden Ticket and at the lucky finder.

'Where is it?' somebody shouted. 'Hold it up so all of us can see it!'

'There it is, there!' someone else shouted. 'He's holding it in his hands! See the gold shining!'

'How did *he* manage to find it, I'd like to know?' a large boy shouted angrily. '*Twenty* bars a day I've been buying for weeks and weeks!'

'Think of all the free stuff he'll be getting too!' another boy said enviously. 'A lifetime supply!'

'He'll need it, the skinny little shrimp!' a girl said, laughing.

Charlie hadn't moved. He hadn't even unwrapped the Golden Ticket from around the chocolate. He was standing very still, holding it tightly with both hands while the crowd pushed and shouted all around him. He felt quite dizzy. There was a peculiar floating sensation coming over him, as though he were floating up in the air like a balloon. His feet didn't seem to be touching the ground at all. He could hear his heart thumping away loudly somewhere in his throat.

At that point, he became aware of a hand resting lightly on his shoulder, and when he looked up, he saw a tall man standing over him. 'Listen,' the man whispered. 'I'll buy it from you. I'll give you fifty pounds. How about it, eh? And I'll give you a new bicycle as well. Okay?'

'Are you *crazy*?' shouted a woman who was standing equally close. 'Why, I'd give him *two hundred* pounds for that ticket! You want to sell that ticket for two hundred pounds, young man?'

'That's *quite* enough of that!' the fat shopkeeper shouted, pushing his way through the crowd and taking Charlie firmly by the arm. 'Leave the kid alone, will you! Make way there! Let him out!' And to Charlie, as he led him to the door, he whispered, 'Don't you let *anybody* have it! Take it straight home, quickly, before you lose it! Run all the way and don't stop till you get there, you understand?'

Charlie nodded.

'You know something,' the fat shopkeeper said,

pausing a moment and smiling at Charlie, 'I have a feeling you needed a break like this. I'm awfully glad you got it. Good luck to you, sonny.'

'Thank you,' Charlie said, and off he went, running through the snow as fast as his legs would go. And as he flew past Mr Willy Wonka's factory, he turned and waved at it and sang out, 'I'll be seeing you! I'll be seeing you soon!' And five minutes later he arrived at his own home.

What It Said on the Golden Ticket

Charlie burst through the front door, shouting, '*Mother! Mother! Mother!*'

Mrs Bucket was in the old grandparents' room, serving them their evening soup.

'*Mother!*' yelled Charlie, rushing in on them like a hurricane. 'Look! I've got it! Look, Mother, look! The last Golden Ticket! It's mine! I found some money in the street and I bought two bars of chocolate and the second one had the Golden Ticket and there were *crowds* of people all around me wanting to see it and the shopkeeper rescued me and I ran all the way home and here I am! *IT'S THE FIFTH GOLDEN TICKET, MOTHER, AND I'VE FOUND IT!*'

Mrs Bucket simply stood and stared, while the four old grandparents, who were sitting up in bed balancing bowls of soup on their laps, all dropped their spoons with a clatter and froze against their pillows.

For about ten seconds there was absolute silence in the room. Nobody dared to speak or move. It was a magic moment.

Then, very softly, Grandpa Joe said, 'You're

pulling our legs, Charlie, aren't you? You're having a little joke?'

'I am *not*!' cried Charlie, rushing up to the bed and holding out the large and beautiful Golden Ticket for him to see.

Grandpa Joe leaned forward and took a close look, his nose almost touching the ticket. The others watched him, waiting for the verdict.

Then very slowly, with a slow and marvellous grin spreading all over his face, Grandpa Joe lifted his head and looked straight at Charlie. The colour was rushing to his cheeks, and his eyes were wide open, shining with joy, and in the centre of each eye, right in the very centre, in the black pupil, a little spark of wild excitement was slowly dancing. Then the old man took a deep breath, and suddenly, with no warning whatsoever, an explosion seemed to take place inside him. He threw up his arms and yelled '*Yippeeeeeeee!*' And at the same time, his long bony body rose up out of the bed and his bowl of soup went flying into the face of Grandma Josephine, and in one fantastic leap, this old fellow of ninety-six and a half, who hadn't been out of bed these last twenty years, jumped on to the floor and started doing a dance of victory in his pyjamas.

'Yippeeeeeeeeee!' he shouted. 'Three cheers for Charlie! Hip, hip, hooray!'

At this point, the door opened, and Mr Bucket walked into the room. He was cold and tired, and he looked it. All day long, he had been shovelling snow in the streets.

'*Cripes!*' he cried. 'What's going on in here?'

It didn't take them long to tell him what had happened.

'I don't believe it!' he said. 'It's not possible.'

'Show him the ticket, Charlie!' shouted Grandpa Joe, who was still dancing around the floor like a dervish in his striped pyjamas. 'Show your father the fifth and last Golden Ticket in the world!'

'Let me see it, Charlie,' Mr Bucket said, collapsing into a chair and holding out his hand. Charlie came forward with the precious document.

It was a very beautiful thing, this Golden Ticket, having been made, so it seemed, from a sheet of pure gold hammered out almost to the thinness of paper. On one side of it, printed by some clever method in jet-black letters, was the invitation itself – from Mr Wonka.

'Read it aloud,' said Grandpa Joe, climbing back into bed again at last. 'Let's all hear exactly what it says.'

Mr Bucket held the lovely Golden Ticket up close to his eyes. His hands were trembling slightly, and he seemed to be overcome by the whole business. He took several deep breaths. Then he cleared his throat, and said, 'All right, I'll read it. Here we go:

'*Greetings to you,* the lucky finder of this Golden Ticket, from Mr Willy Wonka! I shake you warmly by the hand! Tremendous things are in store for you! Many wonderful surprises await you! For now, I do invite you to come to my factory and be my guest for one whole day – you and all others who are lucky enough to find my Golden Tickets. I, Willy Wonka, will conduct you around the factory myself, showing you everything that there is to see, and afterwards, when it is time to leave, you will be escorted home by a procession of large trucks. These trucks, I can promise you, will be loaded with enough delicious eatables to last you and your entire household for many years. If, at any time thereafter, you should run out of supplies, you have only to come back to the factory and show this Golden Ticket, and I shall be happy to refill your cupboard with whatever you want. In this way, you will be able to keep yourself supplied with tasty morsels for the rest of your life. But this is by no means the most exciting thing that will happen on the day of your visit. I am preparing other surprises that are even more marvellous and more fantastic for you and for all my beloved Golden Ticket holders – mystic and marvellous surprises that will entrance, delight, intrigue, astonish, and perplex you beyond measure. In your wildest dreams you could not imagine that such things could happen to you! Just wait and see! And now, here are your instructions: the day I have chosen for the visit is the first day in the month of February. On this day, and on no other, you must come to the factory gates at ten o'clock sharp in the morning. Don't be late! And you are allowed to bring with you either one or two members of your own family to look after you and to ensure that you don't get into mischief. One more thing – be certain to have this ticket with you, otherwise you will not be admitted.

(Signed) Willy Wonka.'

'The first day of *February*!' cried Mrs Bucket. 'But that's *tomorrow*! Today is the last day of January. *I know it is!*'

'Cripes!' said Mr Bucket. 'I think you're right!'

'You're just in time!' shouted Grandpa Joe. 'There's not a moment to lose. You must start making preparations at once! Wash your face, comb your hair, scrub your hands, brush your teeth, blow your nose, cut your nails, polish your shoes, iron your shirt, and for heaven's sake, get all that mud off your pants! You must get ready, my boy! You must get ready for the biggest day of your life!'

'Now don't over-excite yourself, Grandpa,' Mrs Bucket said. 'And don't fluster poor Charlie. We must all try to keep very calm. Now the first thing to decide is this – who is going to go with Charlie to the factory?'

'I will!' shouted Grandpa Joe, leaping out of bed once again. 'I'll take him! I'll look after him! You leave it to me!'

Mrs Bucket smiled at the old man, then she turned to her husband and said, 'How about you, dear? Don't you think *you* ought to go?'

'Well . . .' Mr Bucket said, pausing to think about it, 'no . . . I'm not so sure that I should.'

'But you *must*.'

'There's no *must* about it, my dear,' Mr Bucket said gently. 'Mind you, I'd *love* to go. It'll be tremendously exciting. But on the other hand . . . I believe that the person who really *deserves* to go most of all is Grandpa Joe himself. He seems to

70

know more about it than we do. Provided, of course, that he feels well enough . . .'

'Yippeeeeee!' shouted Grandpa Joe, seizing Charlie by the hands and dancing round the room.

'He certainly *seems* well enough,' Mrs Bucket said, laughing. 'Yes . . . perhaps you're right after all. Perhaps Grandpa Joe should be the one to go with him. I certainly can't go myself and leave the other three old people all alone in bed for a whole day.'

'Hallelujah!' yelled Grandpa Joe. 'Praise the Lord!'

At that point, there came a loud knock on the front door. Mr Bucket went to open it, and the next moment, swarms of newspapermen and photographers were pouring into the house. They had tracked down the finder of the fifth Golden Ticket, and now they all wanted to get the full story for the front pages of the morning papers. For several hours, there was complete pandemonium in the little house, and it must have been nearly midnight before Mr Bucket was able to get rid of them so that Charlie could go to bed.

The Big Day Arrives

The sun was shining brightly on the morning of the big day, but the ground was still white with snow and the air was very cold.

Outside the gates of Wonka's factory, enormous crowds of people had gathered to watch the five lucky ticket holders going in. The excitement was tremendous. It was just before ten o'clock. The crowds were pushing and shouting, and policemen with arms linked were trying to hold them back from the gates.

Right beside the gates, in a small group that was carefully shielded from the crowds by the police, stood the five famous children, together with the grown-ups who had come with them.

The tall bony figure of Grandpa Joe could be seen standing quietly among them, and beside him, holding tightly on to his hand, was little Charlie Bucket himself.

All the children, except Charlie, had both their mothers and fathers with them, and it was a good thing that they had, otherwise the whole party might have got out of hand. They were so eager to get going that their parents were having to hold them back by force to prevent them from climbing over the gates. 'Be patient!' cried the fathers. 'Be still! It's not *time* yet! It's not ten o'clock!'

Behind him, Charlie Bucket could hear the shouts of the people in the crowd as they pushed and fought to get a glimpse of the famous children.

'There's Violet Beauregarde!' he heard someone shouting. 'That's her all right! I can remember her face from the newspapers!'

'And you know what?' somebody else shouted

back. 'She's still chewing that dreadful old piece of gum she's had for three months! You look at her jaws! They're still working on it!'

'Who's the big fat boy?'

'That's Augustus Gloop!'

'So it is!'

'Enormous, isn't he!'

'Fantastic!'

'Who's the kid with a picture of The Lone Ranger stencilled on his windcheater?'

'That's Mike Teavee! He's the television fiend!'

'He must be crazy! Look at all those toy pistols he's got hanging all over him!'

'The one I want to see is Veruca Salt!' shouted another voice in the crowd. 'She's the girl whose father bought up half a million chocolate bars and then made the workers in his peanut factory unwrap every one of them until they found a Golden Ticket! He gives her anything she wants! Absolutely anything! She only has to start screaming for it and she gets it!'

'Dreadful, isn't it?'

'Shocking, I call it!'

'Which do you think is her?'

'That one! Over there on the left! The little girl in the silver mink coat!'

'Which one is Charlie Bucket?'

'Charlie Bucket? He must be that skinny little shrimp standing beside the old fellow who looks like a skeleton. Very close to us. Just there! See him?'

'Why hasn't he got a coat on in this cold weather?'

'Don't ask me. Maybe he can't afford to buy one.'

'Goodness me! He must be freezing!'

Charlie, standing only a few paces away from the speaker, gave Grandpa Joe's hand a squeeze, and the old man looked down at Charlie and smiled.

Somewhere in the distance, a church clock began striking ten.

Very slowly, with a loud creaking of rusty hinges, the great iron gates of the factory began to swing open.

The crowd became suddenly silent. The children stopped jumping about. All eyes were fixed upon the gates.

'*There he is!*' somebody shouted. '*That's him!*'

And so it was!

Mr Willy Wonka

Mr Wonka was standing all alone just inside the open gates of the factory.

And what an extraordinary little man he was!

He had a black top hat on his head.

He wore a tail coat made of a beautiful plum-coloured velvet.

His trousers were bottle green.

His gloves were pearly grey.

And in one hand he carried a fine gold-topped walking cane.

Covering his chin, there was a small, neat, pointed black beard – a goatee. And his eyes – his eyes were most marvellously bright. They seemed to be sparkling and twinkling at you all the time. The whole face, in fact, was alight with fun and laughter.

And oh, how clever he looked! How quick and sharp and full of life! He kept making quick jerky little movements with his head, cocking it this way and that, and taking everything in with those bright twinkling eyes. He was like a squirrel in the quickness of his movements, like a quick clever old squirrel from the park.

Suddenly, he did a funny little skipping dance in the snow, and he spread his arms wide, and he smiled at the five children who were clustered near the gates, and he called out, 'Welcome, my little friends! Welcome to the factory!'

His voice was high and flutey. 'Will you come forward one at a time, please,' he called out, 'and bring your parents. Then show me your Golden Ticket and give me your name. Who's first?'

The big fat boy stepped up. 'I'm Augustus Gloop,' he said.

'Augustus!' cried Mr Wonka, seizing his hand and pumping it up and down with terrific force. 'My *dear* boy, how *good* to see you! Delighted! Charmed! Overjoyed to have you with us! And *these* are your parents? How *nice*! Come in! Come in! That's right! Step through the gates!'

Mr Wonka was clearly just as excited as everybody else.

'My name,' said the next child to go forward, 'is Veruca Salt.'

'My *dear* Veruca! How *do* you do? What a pleasure this is! You *do* have an interesting name, don't you? I always thought that a veruca was a sort of wart that you got on the sole of your foot! But I must be wrong, mustn't I? How pretty you look in that lovely mink coat! I'm so glad you could come! Dear me, this is going to be *such* an exciting day! I *do* hope you enjoy it! I'm sure you *will*! I *know* you will! Your father? How *are* you, Mr Salt? And Mrs Salt? Overjoyed to see you! Yes, the ticket is *quite* in order! Please go in!'

The next two children, Violet Beauregarde and
Mike Teavee, came forward to have their tickets
examined and then to have their arms practically
pumped off their shoulders by the energetic Mr
Wonka.

And last of all, a small nervous voice whispered,
'Charlie Bucket.'

'Charlie!' cried Mr Wonka. 'Well, well, well! So
there you are! You're the one who found your ticket

only yesterday, aren't you? Yes, yes. I read *all* about it in this morning's papers! *Just* in time, my dear boy! I'm so glad! So happy for you! And this? Your grandfather? Delighted to meet you, sir! Overjoyed! Enraptured! Enchanted! All right! Excellent! Is everybody in now? Five children? Yes! Good! Now will you please follow me! Our tour is about to begin! But *do* keep together! *Please* don't wander off by yourselves! I shouldn't like to lose any of you at *this* stage of the proceedings! Oh, dear me, no!'

Charlie glanced back over his shoulder and saw the great iron entrance gates slowly closing behind him. The crowds on the outside were still pushing and shouting. Charlie took a last look at them. Then, as the gates closed with a clang, all sight of the outside world disappeared.

'Here we are!' cried Mr Wonka, trotting along in front of the group. 'Through this big red door, please! *That's* right! It's nice and warm inside! I have to keep it warm inside the factory because of the workers! My workers are used to an *extremely* hot climate! They can't stand the cold! They'd perish if they went outdoors in this weather! They'd freeze to death!'

'But who *are* these workers?' asked Augustus Gloop.

'All in good time, my dear boy!' said Mr Wonka, smiling at Augustus. 'Be patient! You shall see everything as we go along! Are all of you inside? Good! Would you mind closing the door? Thank you!'

Charlie Bucket found himself standing in a long

corridor that stretched away in front of him as far as he could see. The corridor was so wide that a car could easily have been driven along it. The walls were pale pink, the lighting was soft and pleasant.

'How lovely and warm!' whispered Charlie.

'I know. And what a marvellous smell!' answered Grandpa Joe, taking a long deep sniff. All the most wonderful smells in the world seemed to be mixed up in the air around them – the smell of roasting coffee and burnt sugar and melting chocolate and mint and violets and crushed hazelnuts and apple blossom and caramel and lemon peel . . .

And far away in the distance, from the heart of the great factory, came a muffled roar of energy as though some monstrous gigantic machine were spinning its wheels at breakneck speed.

'Now *this,* my dear children,' said Mr Wonka, raising his voice above the noise, 'this is the main corridor. Will you please hang your coats and hats on those pegs over there, and then follow me. *That's* the way! Good! Everyone ready? Come on, then! Here we go!' He trotted off rapidly down the corridor with the tails of his plum-coloured velvet coat flapping behind him, and the visitors all hurried after him.

It was quite a large party of people, when you came to think of it. There were nine grown-ups and five children, fourteen in all. So you can imagine that there was a good deal of pushing and shoving as they hustled and bustled down the passage, trying to keep up with the swift little figure in front of them. 'Come *on*!' cried Mr Wonka. 'Get a move on, please! We'll *never* get round today if you dawdle like this!'

Soon, he turned right off the main corridor into another slightly narrower passage.

Then he turned left.

Then left again.

Then right.

Then left.

Then right.

Then right.

Then left.

The place was like a gigantic rabbit warren, with passages leading this way and that in every direction.

'Don't you let go my hand, Charlie,' whispered Grandpa Joe.

'Notice how all these passages are sloping downwards!' called out Mr Wonka. 'We are now going underground! *All* the most important rooms in my factory are deep down below the surface!'

'Why is that?' somebody asked.

'There wouldn't be *nearly* enough space for them up on top!' answered Mr Wonka. 'These rooms we are going to see are *enormous*! They're larger than football fields! No building in the *world* would be big enough to house them! But down here, underneath the ground, I've got *all* the space I want. There's no limit – so long as I hollow it out.'

Mr Wonka turned right.

He turned left.

He turned right again.

The passages were sloping steeper and steeper downhill now.

Then suddenly, Mr Wonka stopped. In front of him, there was a shiny metal door. The party crowded round. On the door, in large letters, it said:

THE CHOCOLATE ROOM

15

The Chocolate Room

'An important room, this!' cried Mr Wonka, taking a bunch of keys from his pocket and slipping one into the keyhole of the door. '*This* is the nerve centre of the whole factory, the heart of the whole business! And so *beautiful*! I *insist* upon my rooms being beautiful! I can't *abide* ugliness in factories! *In* we go, then! But *do* be careful, my dear children! Don't lose your heads! Don't get over-excited! Keep very calm!'

Mr Wonka opened the door. Five children and nine grown-ups pushed their ways in – and *oh*, what an amazing sight it was that now met their eyes!

They were looking down upon a lovely valley. There were green meadows on either side of the valley, and along the bottom of it there flowed a great brown river.

What is more, there was a tremendous waterfall halfway along the river – a steep cliff over which the water curled and rolled in a solid sheet, and then went crashing down into a boiling churning whirlpool of froth and spray.

Below the waterfall (and this was the most

astonishing sight of all), a whole mass of enormous glass pipes were dangling down into the river from somewhere high up in the ceiling! They really were *enormous,* those pipes. There must have been a dozen of them at least, and they were sucking up the brownish muddy water from the river and carrying it away to goodness knows where. And because they were made of glass, you could see the liquid flowing and bubbling along inside them, and above the noise of the waterfall, you could hear the never-ending suck-suck-sucking sound of the pipes as they did their work.

Graceful trees and bushes were growing along the riverbanks – weeping willows and alders and tall clumps of rhododendrons with their pink and red and mauve blossoms. In the meadows there were thousands of buttercups.

'*There!*' cried Mr Wonka, dancing up and down and pointing his gold-topped cane at the great brown river. 'It's *all* chocolate! Every drop of that river is hot melted chocolate of the finest quality. The *very* finest quality. There's enough chocolate in there to fill *every* bathtub in the *entire* country! *And* all the swimming pools as well! Isn't it *terrific*? And just look at my pipes! They suck up the chocolate and carry it away to all the other rooms in the factory where it is needed! Thousands of gallons an hour, my dear children! Thousands and thousands of gallons!'

The children and their parents were too flabbergasted to speak. They were staggered. They were dumbfounded. They were bewildered and dazzled.

They were completely bowled over by the hugeness of the whole thing. They simply stood and stared.

'The waterfall is *most* important!' Mr Wonka went on. 'It mixes the chocolate! It churns it up! It pounds it and beats it! It makes it light and frothy! No other factory in the world mixes its chocolate by waterfall! But it's the *only* way to do it properly! The *only* way! And do you like my trees?' he cried, pointing with his stick. 'And my lovely bushes? Don't you think they look pretty? I told you I hated ugliness! And of course they are *all* eatable! All made of something different and delicious! And do you like my meadows? Do you like my grass and my buttercups? The grass you are standing on, my dear little ones, is made of a new kind of soft, minty sugar that I've just invented! I call it swudge! Try a blade! Please do! It's delectable!'

Automatically, everybody bent down and picked one blade of grass – everybody, that is, except Augustus Gloop, who took a big handful.

And Violet Beauregarde, before tasting her blade of grass, took the piece of world-record-breaking chewing-gum out of her mouth and stuck it carefully behind her ear.

'Isn't it *wonderful*!' whispered Charlie. 'Hasn't it got a wonderful taste, Grandpa?'

'I could eat the whole *field*!' said Grandpa Joe, grinning with delight. 'I could go around on all fours like a cow and eat every blade of grass in the field!'

'Try a buttercup!' cried Mr Wonka. 'They're even *nicer*!'

Suddenly, the air was filled with screams of excitement. The screams came from Veruca Salt. She was pointing frantically to the other side of the river. '*Look!* Look over there!' she screamed. 'What *is* it? He's moving! He's walking! It's a little *person*! It's a little *man*! Down there below the waterfall!'

Everybody stopped picking buttercups and stared across the river.

'*She's right, Grandpa!*' cried Charlie. 'It *is* a little man! Can you *see* him?'

'I see him, Charlie!' said Grandpa Joe excitedly.

And now everybody started shouting at once.

'There's *two* of them!'

'My gosh, so there is!'

'There's more than two! There's one, two, three, four, five!'

'What are they *doing*?'

'Where do they *come* from?'

'Who *are* they?'

Children and parents alike rushed down to the edge of the river to get a closer look.

'Aren't they *fantastic*!'

'No higher than my knee!'

'Look at their funny long hair!'

The tiny men – they were no larger than medium-sized dolls – had stopped what they were doing, and now they were staring back across the river at the visitors. One of them pointed towards the children, and then he whispered something to the other four, and all five of them burst into peals of laughter.

'But they can't be *real* people,' Charlie said.

'Of course they're real people,' Mr Wonka answered. 'They're Oompa-Loompas.'

The Oompa-Loompas

'Oompa-Loompas!' everyone said at once. '*Oompa-Loompas!*'

'Imported direct from Loompaland,' said Mr Wonka proudly.

'There's no such place,' said Mrs Salt.

'Excuse me, dear lady, but . . .'

'*Mr Wonka,*' cried Mrs Salt. 'I'm a teacher of geography . . .'

'Then you'll know all about it,' said Mr Wonka. 'And oh, what a terrible country it is! Nothing but thick jungles infested by the most dangerous beasts in the world – hornswogglers and snozzwangers and those terrible wicked whangdoodles. A whangdoodle would eat ten Oompa-Loompas for breakfast and come galloping back for a second helping. When I went out there, I found the little Oompa-Loompas living in tree houses. They *had* to live in tree houses to escape from the whangdoodles and the hornswogglers and the snozzwangers. And they were living on green caterpillars, and the caterpillars tasted revolting, and the Oompa-Loompas spent every moment of their days climbing through the treetops looking for other things to mash up

with the caterpillars to make them taste better —
red beetles, for instance, and eucalyptus leaves,
and the bark of the bong-bong tree, all of them
beastly, but not quite so beastly as the caterpillars.
Poor little Oompa-Loompas! The one food that
they longed for more than any other was the cacao
bean. But they couldn't get it. An Oompa-Loompa
was lucky if he found three or four cacao beans a
year. But oh, how they craved them. They used to
dream about cacao beans all night and talk about
them all day. You had only to *mention* the word
"cacao" to an Oompa-Loompa and he would start
dribbling at the mouth. The cacao bean,' Mr
Wonka continued, 'which grows on the cacao tree,
happens to be *the thing* from which all chocolate is
made. You cannot make chocolate without the

cacao bean. The cacao bean *is* chocolate. I myself use billions of cacao beans every week in this factory. And so, my dear children, as soon as I discovered that the Oompa-Loompas were crazy about this particular food, I climbed up to their tree-house village and poked my head in through the door of the tree house belonging to the leader of the tribe. The poor little fellow, looking thin and starved, was sitting there trying to eat a bowl full of mashed-up green caterpillars without being sick. "Look here," I said (speaking not in English, of course, but in Oompa-Loompish), "look here, if you and all your people will come back to my country and live in my factory, you can have *all* the cacao beans you want! I've got mountains of them in my storehouses! You can have cacao beans for every meal! You can gorge yourselves silly on them! I'll even pay your wages in cacao beans if you wish!"

'"You really mean it?" asked the Oompa-Loompa leader, leaping up from his chair.

'"Of course I mean it," I said. "And you can have chocolate as well. Chocolate tastes even better than cacao beans because it's got milk and sugar added."

'The little man gave a great whoop of joy and threw his bowl of mashed caterpillars right out of the tree-house window. "It's a deal!" he cried. "Come on! Let's go!"

'So I shipped them all over here, every man, woman, and child in the Oompa-Loompa tribe. It was easy. I smuggled them over in large packing cases with holes in them, and they all got here safely. They are wonderful workers. They all speak English now. They love dancing and music. They are always making up songs. I expect you will hear a good deal of singing today from time to time. I must warn you, though, that they are rather mischievous. They like jokes. They still wear the same kind of clothes they wore in the jungle. They insist upon that. The men, as you can see for yourselves across the river, wear only deerskins. The women wear leaves, and the children wear nothing at all. The women use fresh leaves every day . . .'

'*Daddy!*' shouted Veruca Salt (the girl who got everything she wanted). '*Daddy!* I want an Oompa-Loompa! I want you to get me an Oompa-Loompa! I want an Oompa-Loompa right away! I want to take it home with me! Go on, Daddy! Get me an Oompa-Loompa!'

'Now, now, my pet!' her father said to her, 'we mustn't interrupt Mr Wonka.'

'*But I want an Oompa-Loompa!*' screamed Veruca.

'All *right*, Veruca, all *right*. But I can't get it for you this second. Please be patient. I'll see you have one before the day is out.'

'Augustus!' shouted Mrs Gloop. 'Augustus, sweetheart, I don't think you had better do *that*.' Augustus Gloop, as you might have guessed, had quietly sneaked down to the edge of the river, and he was now kneeling on the riverbank, scooping hot melted chocolate into his mouth as fast as he could.

Augustus Gloop Goes up the Pipe

When Mr Wonka turned round and saw what Augustus Gloop was doing, he cried out, 'Oh, no! *Please*, Augustus, *please*! I beg of you not to do that. My chocolate must be untouched by human hands!'

'Augustus!' called out Mrs Gloop. 'Didn't you hear what the man said? Come away from that river at once!'

'This stuff is fabulous!' said Augustus, taking not the slightest notice of his mother or Mr Wonka. 'Gosh, I need a bucket to drink it properly!'

'Augustus,' cried Mr Wonka, hopping up and down and waggling his stick in the air, 'you *must* come away. You are dirtying my chocolate!'

'Augustus!' cried Mrs Gloop.

'Augustus!' cried Mr Gloop.

But Augustus was deaf to everything except the call of his enormous stomach. He was now lying full length on the ground with his head far out over the river, lapping up the chocolate like a dog.

'Augustus!' shouted Mrs Gloop. 'You'll be giving that nasty cold of yours to about a million people all over the country!'

'Be careful, Augustus!' shouted Mr Gloop. 'You're leaning too far out!'

Mr Gloop was absolutely right. For suddenly there was a shriek, and then a splash, and into the river went Augustus Gloop, and in one second he had disappeared under the brown surface.

'Save him!' screamed Mrs Gloop, going white in the face, and waving her umbrella about. 'He'll drown! He can't swim a yard! Save him! Save him!'

'Good heavens, woman,' said Mr Gloop, 'I'm not diving in there! I've got my best suit on!'

Augustus Gloop's face came up again to the surface, painted brown with chocolate. 'Help! Help! Help!' he yelled. 'Fish me out!'

'Don't just *stand* there!' Mrs Gloop screamed at Mr Gloop. '*Do* something!'

'I *am* doing something!' said Mr Gloop, who was now taking off his jacket and getting ready to dive into the chocolate. But while he was doing this, the wretched boy was being sucked closer and

closer towards the mouth of one of the great pipes that was dangling down into the river. Then all at once, the powerful suction took hold of him completely, and he was pulled under the surface and then into the mouth of the pipe.

The crowd on the riverbank waited breathlessly to see where he would come out.

'*There he goes!*' somebody shouted, pointing upwards.

And sure enough, because the pipe was made of glass, Augustus Gloop could be clearly seen shooting up inside it, head first, like a torpedo.

'Help! Murder! Police!' screamed Mrs Gloop. 'Augustus, come back at once! Where are you going?'

'It's a wonder to me,' said Mr Gloop, 'how that pipe is big enough for him to go through it.'

'It *isn't* big enough!' said Charlie Bucket. 'Oh dear, look! He's slowing down!'

'So he is!' said Grandpa Joe.

'He's going to stick!' said Charlie.

'I think he is!' said Grandpa Joe.

'By golly, he *has* stuck!' said Charlie.

'It's his stomach that's done it!' said Mr Gloop.

'He's blocked the whole pipe!' said Grandpa Joe.

'Smash the pipe!' yelled Mrs Gloop, still waving her umbrella. 'Augustus, come out of there at once!'

The watchers below could see the chocolate swishing around the boy in the pipe, and they could see it building up behind him in a solid mass, pushing against the blockage. The pressure was terrific.

Something had to give. Something did give, and that something was Augustus. *WHOOF!* Up he shot again like a bullet in the barrel of a gun.

'He's disappeared!' yelled Mrs Gloop. 'Where does that pipe go to? Quick! Call the fire brigade!'

'Keep calm!' cried Mr Wonka. 'Keep calm, my dear lady, keep calm. There is no danger! No danger whatsoever! Augustus has gone on a little journey, that's all. A most interesting little journey. But he'll come out of it just fine, you wait and see.'

'How can he possibly come out just fine!' snapped Mrs Gloop. 'He'll be made into marshmallows in five seconds!'

'Impossible!' cried Mr Wonka. 'Unthinkable! Inconceivable! Absurd! He could never be made into marshmallows!'

'And why not, may I ask?' shouted Mrs Gloop.

'Because that pipe doesn't go anywhere near it! That pipe – the one Augustus went up – happens to lead directly to the room where I make a most delicious kind of strawberry-flavoured chocolate-coated fudge . . .'

'Then he'll be made into strawberry-flavoured chocolate-coated fudge!' screamed Mrs Gloop. 'My poor Augustus! They'll be selling him by the pound all over the country tomorrow morning!'

'Quite right,' said Mr Gloop.

'I know I'm right,' said Mrs Gloop.

'It's beyond a joke,' said Mr Gloop.

'Mr Wonka doesn't seem to think so!' cried Mrs Gloop. 'Just look at him! He's laughing his head off! How *dare* you laugh like that when my boy's just gone up the pipe! You monster!' she shrieked, pointing her umbrella at Mr Wonka as though she were going to run him through. 'You think it's a joke, do you? You think that sucking my boy up into your Fudge Room like that is just one great big colossal joke?'

'He'll be perfectly safe,' said Mr Wonka, giggling slightly.

'He'll be chocolate fudge!' shrieked Mrs Gloop.

'Never!' cried Mr Wonka.

'Of course he will!' shrieked Mrs Gloop.

'I wouldn't allow it!' cried Mr Wonka.

'And why not?' shrieked Mrs Gloop.

'Because the taste would be terrible,' said Mr Wonka. 'Just imagine it! Augustus-flavoured chocolate-coated Gloop! No one would buy it.'

'They most certainly would!' cried Mr Gloop indignantly.

'I don't want to think about it!' shrieked Mrs Gloop.

'Nor do I,' said Mr Wonka. 'And I do promise you, madam, that your darling boy is perfectly safe.'

'If he's perfectly safe, then where is he?' snapped Mrs Gloop. 'Lead me to him this instant!'

Mr Wonka turned around and clicked his fingers sharply, *click, click, click,* three times. Immediately, an Oompa-Loompa appeared, as if from nowhere, and stood beside him.

The Oompa-Loompa bowed and smiled, show-ing beautiful white teeth. His skin was rosy-white, his long hair was golden-brown, and the top of his head came just above the height of Mr Wonka's knee. He wore the usual deerskin slung over his shoulder.

'Now listen to me!' said Mr Wonka, looking down at the tiny man. 'I want you to take Mr and Mrs Gloop up to the Fudge Room and help them to find their son, Augustus. He's just gone up the pipe.'

The Oompa-Loompa took one look at Mrs Gloop and exploded into peals of laughter.

'Oh, do be quiet!' said Mr Wonka. 'Control yourself! Pull yourself together! Mrs Gloop doesn't think it's at all funny!'

'You can say that again!' said Mrs Gloop.

'Go straight to the Fudge Room,' Mr Wonka said to the Oompa-Loompa, 'and when you get there, take a long stick and start poking around inside the big chocolate-mixing barrel. I'm almost certain you'll find him in there. But you'd better look sharp! You'll have to hurry! If you leave him in the chocolate-mixing barrel too long, he's liable to get poured out into the fudge boiler, and that really *would* be a disaster, wouldn't it? My fudge would become *quite* uneatable!'

Mrs Gloop let out a shriek of fury.

'I'm joking,' said Mr Wonka, giggling madly behind his beard. 'I didn't mean it. Forgive me. I'm so sorry. Good-bye, Mrs Gloop! And Mr Gloop! Good-bye! I'll see you later . . .'

As Mr and Mrs Gloop and their tiny escort hurried away, the five Oompa-Loompas on the far side of the river suddenly began hopping and dancing about and beating wildly upon a number of very small drums. 'Augustus Gloop!' they chanted. 'Augustus Gloop! Augustus Gloop! Augustus Gloop!'

'Grandpa!' cried Charlie. 'Listen to them, Grandpa! What *are* they doing?'

'Ssshh!' whispered Grandpa Joe. 'I think they're going to sing us a song!'

'*Augustus Gloop!*' chanted the Oompa-Loompas.
'*Augustus Gloop! Augustus Gloop!*
The great big greedy nincompoop!
How long could we allow this beast
To gorge and guzzle, feed and feast
On everything he wanted to?
Great Scott! It simply wouldn't do!
However long this pig might live,
We're positive he'd never give
Even the smallest bit of fun
Or happiness to anyone.
So what we do in cases such
As this, we use the gentle touch,
And carefully we take the brat
And turn him into something that
Will give great pleasure to us all –
A doll, for instance, or a ball,
Or marbles or a rocking horse.
But this revolting boy, of course,
Was so unutterably vile,
So greedy, foul, and infantile,
He left a most disgusting taste
Inside our mouths, and so in haste
We chose a thing that, come what may,
Would take the nasty taste away.
"*Come on!*" *we cried. "The time is ripe*
To send him shooting up the pipe!
He has to go! It has to be!"
And very soon, he's going to see
Inside the room to which he's gone
Some funny things are going on.
But don't, dear children, be alarmed;

Augustus Gloop will not be harmed,
Although, of course, we must admit
He will be altered quite a bit.
He'll be quite changed from what he's been,
When he goes through the fudge machine:
Slowly, the wheels go round and round,
The cogs begin to grind and pound;
A hundred knives go slice, slice, slice;
We add some sugar, cream, and spice;
We boil him for a minute more,
Until we're absolutely sure
That all the greed and all the gall
Is boiled away for once and all.
Then out he comes! And now! By grace!
A miracle has taken place!
This boy, who only just before
Was loathed by men from shore to shore,
This greedy brute, this louse's ear,
Is loved by people everywhere!
For who could hate or bear a grudge
Against a luscious bit of fudge?"

'I *told* you they loved singing!' cried Mr Wonka. 'Aren't they delightful? Aren't they charming? But you mustn't believe a word they said. It's all non-sense, every bit of it!'

'Are the Oompa-Loompas really joking, Grandpa?' asked Charlie.

'Of course they're joking,' answered Grandpa Joe. 'They *must* be joking. At least, I hope they're joking. Don't you?'

Down the Chocolate River

'Off we go!' cried Mr Wonka. 'Hurry up, every-body! Follow me to the next room! And please don't worry about Augustus Gloop. He's bound to come out in the wash. They always do. We shall have to make the next part of the journey by boat! Here she comes! Look!'

A steamy mist was rising up now from the great warm chocolate river, and out of the mist there appeared suddenly a most fantastic pink boat. It was a large open row boat with a tall front and a tall back (like a Viking boat of old), and it was of such a shining sparkling glistening pink colour that the whole thing looked as though it were made of bright, pink glass. There were many oars on either side of it, and as the boat came closer, the watchers on the riverbank could see that the oars were being pulled by masses of Oompa-Loompas – at least ten of them to each oar.

'This is my private yacht!' cried Mr Wonka, beaming with pleasure. 'I made her by hollowing out an enormous boiled sweet! Isn't she beautiful! See how she comes cutting through the river!'

The gleaming pink boiled-sweet boat glided up

to the riverbank. One hundred Oompa-Loompas rested on their oars and stared up at the visitors. Then suddenly, for some reason best known to themselves, they all burst into shrieks of laughter.

'What's so funny?' asked Violet Beauregarde.

'Oh, don't worry about *them*!' cried Mr Wonka. 'They're always laughing! They think everything's a colossal joke! Jump into the boat, all of you! Come on! Hurry up!'

As soon as everyone was safely in, the Oompa-Loompas pushed the boat away from the bank and began to row swiftly downriver.

'Hey, there! Mike Teavee!' shouted Mr Wonka. 'Please do not lick the boat with your tongue! It'll only make it sticky!'

'Daddy,' said Veruca Salt, 'I want a boat like this! I want you to buy me a big pink boiled-sweet boat exactly like Mr Wonka's! And I want lots of Oompa-Loompas to row me about, and I want a chocolate river and I want . . . I want . . .'

'She wants a good kick in the pants,' whispered Grandpa Joe to Charlie. The old man was sitting in the back of the boat and little Charlie Bucket was right beside him. Charlie was holding tightly on to his grandfather's bony old hand. He was in a whirl of excitement. Everything that he had seen so far – the great chocolate river, the water-fall, the huge sucking pipes, the minty sugar meadows, the Oompa-Loompas, the beautiful pink boat, and most of all, Mr Willy Wonka himself – had been so astonishing that he began to wonder

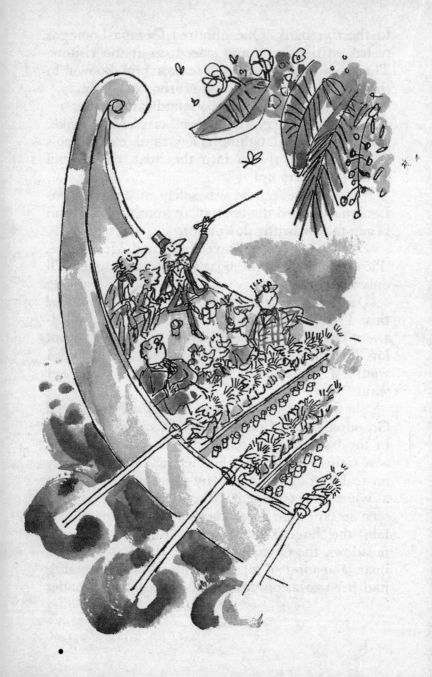

whether there could possibly be any more astonishments left. Where were they going now? What were they going to see? And what in the world was going to happen in the next room?

'Isn't it marvellous?' said Grandpa Joe, grinning at Charlie.

Charlie nodded and smiled up at the old man.

Suddenly, Mr Wonka, who was sitting on Charlie's other side, reached down into the bottom of the boat, picked up a large mug, dipped it into the river, filled it with chocolate, and handed it to Charlie. 'Drink this,' he said. 'It'll do you good! You look starved to death!'

Then Mr Wonka filled a second mug and gave it to Grandpa Joe. 'You, too,' he said. 'You look like a skeleton! What's the matter? Hasn't there been anything to eat in your house lately?'

'Not much,' said Grandpa Joe.

Charlie put the mug to his lips, and as the rich warm creamy chocolate ran down his throat into his empty tummy, his whole body from head to toe began to tingle with pleasure, and a feeling of intense happiness spread over him.

'You like it?' asked Mr Wonka.

'Oh, it's wonderful!' Charlie said.

'The creamiest loveliest chocolate I've ever tasted!' said Grandpa Joe, smacking his lips.

'That's because it's been mixed by waterfall,' Mr Wonka told him.

The boat sped on down the river. The river was getting narrower. There was some kind of a dark tunnel ahead – a great round tunnel that looked like an enormous pipe – and the river was running right into the tunnel. And so was the boat! 'Row on!' shouted Mr Wonka, jumping up and waving his stick in the air. 'Full speed ahead!' And with the Oompa-Loompas rowing faster than ever, the boat shot into the pitch-dark tunnel, and all the passengers screamed with excitement.

'How can they see where they're going?' shrieked Violet Beauregarde in the darkness.

'There's no knowing where they're going!' cried Mr Wonka, hooting with laughter.

> *'There's no earthly way of knowing*
> *Which direction they are going!*
> *There's no knowing where they're rowing,*
> *Or which way the river's flowing!*
> *Not a speck of light is showing,*
> *So the danger must be growing,*
> *For the rowers keep on rowing,*
> *And they're certainly not showing*
> *Any signs that they are slowing . . . '*

'He's gone off his rocker!' shouted one of the fathers, aghast, and the other parents joined in the chorus of frightened shouting. 'He's crazy!' they shouted.

'He's balmy!'
'He's nutty!'
'He's screwy!'
'He's batty!'
'He's dippy!'
'He's dotty!'

'He's daffy!'

'He's goofy!'

'He's beany!'

'He's buggy!'

'He's wacky!'

'He's loony!'

'No, he is *not*!' said Grandpa Joe.

'Switch on the lights!' shouted Mr Wonka. And suddenly, on came the lights and the whole tunnel was brilliantly lit up, and Charlie could see that they were indeed inside a gigantic pipe, and the great upward-curving walls of the pipe were pure white and spotlessly clean. The river of chocolate was flowing very fast inside the pipe, and the Oompa-Loompas were all rowing like mad, and the boat was rocketing along at a furious pace. Mr Wonka was jumping up and down in the back of the boat and calling to the rowers to row faster and faster still. He seemed to love the sensation of whizzing through a white tunnel in a pink boat on a chocolate river, and he clapped his hands and laughed and kept glancing at his passengers to see if they were enjoying it as much as he.

'Look, Grandpa!' cried Charlie. 'There's a door in the wall!' It was a green door and it was set into the wall of the tunnel just above the level of the river. As they flashed past it there was just enough time to read the writing on the door: STORE-ROOM NUMBER 54, it said. ALL THE CREAMS – DAIRY CREAM, WHIPPED CREAM, VIOLET CREAM, COFFEE CREAM, PINEAPPLE CREAM, VANILLA

CREAM, AND HAIR CREAM.

'Hair cream?' cried Mike Teavee. 'You don't use *hair cream*?'

'Row on!' shouted Mr Wonka. 'There's no time to answer silly questions!'

They streaked past a black door. STORE-ROOM NUMBER 71, it said on it. WHIPS – ALL SHAPES AND SIZES.

'*Whips!*' cried Veruca Salt. 'What on earth do you use whips for?'

'For whipping cream, of course,' said Mr Wonka. 'How can you whip cream without whips? Whipped cream isn't whipped cream at all unless it's been whipped with whips. Just as a poached egg isn't a poached egg unless it's been stolen from the woods in the dead of night! Row on, please!'

They passed a yellow door on which it said: STOREROOM NUMBER 77 – ALL THE BEANS, CACAO BEANS, COFFEE BEANS, JELLY BEANS, AND HAS BEANS.

'*Has beans?*' cried Violet Beauregarde.

'You're one yourself!' said Mr Wonka. 'There's no time for arguing! Press on, press on!' But five seconds later, when a bright red door came into sight ahead, he suddenly waved his gold-topped cane in the air and shouted, 'Stop the boat!'

The Inventing Room –
Everlasting Gobstoppers and
Hair Toffee

When Mr Wonka shouted 'Stop the boat!' the Oompa-Loompas jammed their oars into the river and backed water furiously. The boat stopped.

The Oompa-Loompas guided the boat alongside the red door. On the door it said, INVENTING ROOM – PRIVATE – KEEP OUT. Mr Wonka took a key from his pocket, leaned over the side of the boat, and put the key in the keyhole.

'*This* is the most important room in the entire factory!' he said. 'All my most secret new inventions are cooking and simmering in here! Old Fickelgruber would give his front teeth to be allowed inside just for three minutes! So would Prodnose and Slugworth and all the other rotten chocolate makers! But now, listen to me! I want no messing about when you go in! No touching, no meddling, and no tasting! Is that agreed?'

'Yes, yes!' the children cried. 'We won't touch a thing!'

'Up to now,' Mr Wonka said, 'nobody else, not even an Oompa-Loompa, has ever been allowed in here!' He opened the door and stepped out of the boat into the room. The four children and their parents all scrambled after him.

'Don't touch!' shouted Mr Wonka. 'And don't knock anything over!'

Charlie Bucket stared around the gigantic room in which he now found himself. The place was like a witch's kitchen! All about him black metal pots were boiling and bubbling on huge stoves, and kettles were hissing and pans were sizzling, and strange iron machines were clanking and spluttering, and there were pipes running all over the ceiling and walls, and the whole place was filled with smoke and steam and delicious rich smells.

Mr Wonka himself had suddenly become even more excited than usual, and anyone could see that this was the room he loved best of all. He was hopping about among the saucepans and the machines like a child among his Christmas presents, not knowing which thing to look at first. He lifted the lid from a huge pot and took a sniff; then he rushed over and dipped a finger into a barrel of sticky yellow stuff and had a taste; then he skipped across to one of the machines and turned half a dozen knobs this way and that; then he peered anxiously through the glass door of a gigantic oven, rubbing his hands and cackling with delight at what he saw inside. Then he ran over to another machine, a small shiny affair that kept going *phut-phut-phut-phut-phut,* and every time it went *phut,* a large green marble dropped out of it into a basket on the floor. At least it looked like a marble.

'Everlasting Gobstoppers!' cried Mr Wonka proudly. 'They're completely new! I am inventing them for children who are given very little pocket money. You can put an Everlasting Gobstopper in your mouth and you can suck it and suck it and suck it and suck it and it will *never* get any smaller!'

'It's like gum!' cried Violet Beauregarde.

'It is *not* like gum,' Mr Wonka said. 'Gum is for chewing, and if you tried chewing one of these Gobstoppers here you'd break your teeth off! And they *never* get any smaller! They *never* disappear! *NEVER!* At least I don't think they do. There's one of them being tested this very moment in the Testing Room next door. An Oompa-Loompa is sucking it. He's been sucking it for very nearly a year now without stopping, and it's still just as good as ever!

'Now, over here,' Mr Wonka went on, skipping excitedly across the room to the opposite wall, 'over here I am inventing a completely new line in toffees!' He stopped beside a large saucepan. The saucepan was full of a thick gooey purplish treacle, boiling and bubbling. By standing on his toes, little Charlie could just see inside it.

'That's Hair Toffee!' cried Mr Wonka. 'You eat just one tiny bit of that, and in exactly half an hour a brand-new luscious thick silky beautiful crop of hair will start growing out all over the top of your head! And a moustache! And a beard!'

'A beard!' cried Veruca Salt. 'Who wants a beard, for heaven's sake?'

'It would suit you very well,' said Mr Wonka,

'but unfortunately the mixture is not quite right yet. I've got it too strong. It works too well. I tried it on an Oompa-Loompa yesterday in the Testing Room and immediately a huge black beard started shooting out of his chin, and the beard grew so fast that soon it was trailing all over the floor in a thick hairy carpet. It was growing faster than we could cut it! In the end we had to use a lawn mower to keep it in check! But I'll get the mixture right soon! And when I do, then there'll be no excuse any more for little boys and girls going about with bald heads!'

'But Mr Wonka,' said Mike Teavee, 'little boys and girls never *do* go about with . . .'

'Don't argue, my dear child, *please* don't argue!' cried Mr Wonka. 'It's such a waste of precious time! Now, over *here,* if you will all step this way, I will show you something that I am terrifically proud of. Oh, do be careful! Don't knock anything over! Stand back!'

The Great Gum Machine

Mr Wonka led the party over to a gigantic machine that stood in the very centre of the Inventing Room. It was a mountain of gleaming metal that towered high above the children and their parents. Out of the very top of it there sprouted hundreds and hundreds of thin glass tubes, and the glass tubes all curled downwards and came together in a bunch and hung suspended over an enormous round tub as big as a bath.

'Here we go!' cried Mr Wonka, and he pressed three different buttons on the side of the machine. A second later, a mighty rumbling sound came from inside it, and the whole machine began to shake most frighteningly, and steam began hissing out of it all over, and then suddenly the watchers noticed that runny stuff was pouring down the insides of all the hundreds of little glass tubes and squirting out into the great tub below. And in every single tube the runny stuff was of a different colour, so that all the colours of the rainbow (and many others as well) came sloshing and splashing into the tub. It was a lovely sight. And when the tub was nearly full, Mr Wonka pressed another button, and immediately the runny stuff disappeared, and a whizzing whirring noise took its place; and then a giant whizzer started whizzing round inside the enormous tub, mixing up all the different coloured liquids like an ice-cream soda. Gradually, the mixture began to froth. It became frothier and frothier, and it turned from blue to white to green to brown to yellow, then back to blue again.

'Watch!' said Mr Wonka.

Click went the machine, and the whizzer stopped whizzing. And now there came a sort of sucking noise, and very quickly all the blue frothy mixture in the huge basin was sucked back into the stomach of the machine. There was a moment of silence. Then a few queer rumblings were heard. Then silence again. Then suddenly, the machine let out a monstrous mighty groan, and at the same moment a tiny drawer (no bigger than the drawer in a slot machine) popped out of the side of the machine, and in the drawer there lay something so small and thin and grey that everyone thought it must be a mistake. The thing looked like a little strip of grey cardboard.

The children and their parents stared at the little grey strip lying in the drawer.

'You mean that's *all*?' said Mike Teavee, disgusted.

'That's all,' answered Mr Wonka, gazing proudly at the result. 'Don't you know what it is?'

There was a pause. Then suddenly, Violet Beauregarde, the silly gum-chewing girl, let out a yell of excitement. 'By gum, it's *gum*!' she shrieked. 'It's a stick of chewing-gum!'

'Right you are!' cried Mr Wonka, slapping Violet hard on the back. 'It's a stick of gum! It's a stick of the most *amazing* and *fabulous* and *sensational* gum in the world!'

Good-bye Violet

'This gum,' Mr Wonka went on, 'is my latest, my greatest, my most fascinating invention! It's a chewing-gum meal! It's . . . it's . . . it's . . . That tiny little strip of gum lying there is a whole three-course dinner all by itself!'

'What sort of nonsense is this?' said one of the fathers.

'My dear sir!' cried Mr Wonka, 'when I start selling this gum in the shops it will change *everything*! It will be the end of all kitchens and all cooking! There will be no more shopping to do! No more buying of meat and groceries! There'll be no knives and forks at mealtimes! No plates! No washing up! No rubbish! No mess! Just a little strip of Wonka's magic chewing-gum – and that's all you'll ever need at breakfast, lunch, and supper! This piece of gum I've just made happens to be tomato soup, roast beef, and blueberry pie, but you can have almost anything you want!'

'What *do* you mean, it's tomato soup, roast beef, and blueberry pie?' said Violet Beauregarde.

'If you were to start chewing it,' said Mr Wonka, 'then that is exactly what you would get on the menu. It's absolutely amazing! You can actually *feel* the food going down your throat and into your tummy! And you can taste it perfectly! And it fills you up! It satisfies you! It's terrific!'

'It's utterly impossible,' said Veruca Salt.

'Just so long as it's gum,' shouted Violet Beauregarde, 'just so long as it's a piece of gum and I can chew it, then *that's* for me!' And quickly she took her own world-record piece of chewing-gum out of her mouth and stuck it behind her left ear. 'Come on, Mr Wonka,' she said, 'hand over this magic gum of yours and we'll see if the thing works.'

'Now, Violet,' said Mrs Beauregarde, her mother; 'don't let's do anything silly, Violet.'

'I want the gum!' Violet said obstinately. 'What's so silly?'

'I would rather you didn't take it,' Mr Wonka told her gently. 'You see, I haven't got it *quite right* yet. There are still one or two things . . .'

'Oh, to blazes with that!' said Violet, and suddenly, before Mr Wonka could stop her, she shot out a fat hand and grabbed the stick of gum out of the little drawer and popped it into her mouth. At once, her huge, well-trained jaws started chewing away on it like a pair of tongs.

'Don't!' said Mr Wonka.

'Fabulous!' shouted Violet. 'It's tomato soup! It's hot and creamy and delicious! I can feel it running down my throat!'

'Stop!' said Mr Wonka. 'The gum isn't ready yet! It's not right!'

'Of course it's right!' said Violet. 'It's working beautifully! Oh my, what lovely soup this is!'

'Spit it out!' said Mr Wonka.

'It's changing!' shouted Violet, chewing and grinning both at the same time. 'The second course is coming up! It's roast beef! It's tender and juicy! Oh boy, what a flavour! The baked potato is marvellous, too! It's got a crispy skin and it's all filled with butter inside!'

'But how *in*-teresting, Violet,' said Mrs Beauregarde. 'You are a clever girl.'

'Keep chewing, baby!' said Mr Beauregarde. 'Keep right on chewing! This is a great day for the Beauregardes! Our little girl is the first person in the world to have a chewing-gum meal!'

Everybody was watching Violet Beauregarde as she stood there chewing this extraordinary gum. Little Charlie Bucket was staring at her absolutely spellbound, watching her huge rubbery lips as they pressed and unpressed with the chewing, and Grandpa Joe stood beside him, gaping at the girl. Mr Wonka was wringing his hands and saying, 'No, no, no, no, no! It isn't ready for eating! It isn't right! You mustn't do it!'

'Blueberry pie and cream!' shouted Violet. 'Here it comes! Oh my, it's perfect! It's beautiful! It's . . . it's exactly as though I'm swallowing it! It's as though I'm chewing and swallowing great big spoonfuls of the most marvellous blueberry pie in the world!'

'Good heavens, girl!' shrieked Mrs Beauregarde suddenly, staring at Violet, 'what's happening to your nose!'

'Oh, be quiet, mother, and let me finish!' said Violet.

'It's turning blue!' screamed Mrs Beauregarde. 'Your nose is turning blue as a blueberry!'

'Your mother is right!' shouted Mr Beauregarde. 'Your whole nose has gone purple!'

'What *do* you mean?' said Violet, still chewing away.

'Your cheeks!' screamed Mrs Beauregarde. 'They're turning blue as well! So is your chin! Your whole face is turning blue!'

'Spit that gum out at once!' ordered Mr Beauregarde.

'Mercy! Save us!' yelled Mrs Beauregarde. 'The girl's going blue and purple all over! Even her hair is changing colour! Violet, you're turning violet, Violet! What *is* happening to you?'

'I *told* you I hadn't got it quite right,' sighed Mr Wonka, shaking his head sadly.

'I'll say you haven't!' cried Mrs Beauregarde. 'Just look at the girl now!'

Everybody was staring at Violet. And what a terrible, peculiar sight she was! Her face and hands and legs and neck, in fact the skin all over her body, as well as her great big mop of curly hair, had turned a brilliant, purplish-blue, the colour of blueberry juice!

'It always goes wrong when we come to the dessert,' sighed Mr Wonka. 'It's the blueberry pie that does it. But I'll get it right one day, you wait and see.'

'Violet,' screamed Mrs Beauregarde, 'you're swelling up!'

'I feel sick,' Violet said.

'You're swelling up!' screamed Mrs Beauregarde again.

'I feel most peculiar!' gasped Violet.

'I'm not surprised!' said Mr Beauregarde.

'Great heavens, girl!' screeched Mrs Beauregarde. 'You're blowing up like a balloon!'

'Like a blueberry,' said Mr Wonka.

'Call a doctor!' shouted Mr Beauregarde.

'Prick her with a pin!' said one of the other fathers.

'Save her!' cried Mrs Beauregarde, wringing her hands.

But there was no saving her now. Her body was swelling up and changing shape at such a rate that within a minute it had turned into nothing less than an enormous round blue ball – a gigantic blueberry, in fact – and all that remained of Violet Beauregarde herself was a tiny pair of legs and a tiny pair of arms sticking out of the great round fruit and little head on top.

'It *always* happens like that,' sighed Mr Wonka. 'I've tried it twenty times in the Testing Room on twenty Oompa-Loompas, and every one of them finished up as a blueberry. It's most annoying. I just can't understand it.'

'But I don't want a blueberry for a daughter!' yelled Mrs Beauregarde. 'Put her back to what she was this instant!'

Mr Wonka clicked his fingers, and ten Oompa-Loompas appeared immediately at his side.

'Roll Miss Beauregarde into the boat,' he said to them, 'and take her along to the Juicing Room at once.'

'The *Juicing Room*?' cried Mrs Beauregarde. 'What are they going to do to her there?'

'Squeeze her,' said Mr Wonka. 'We've got to squeeze the juice out of her immediately. After that, we'll just have to see how she comes out. But don't worry, my dear Mrs Beauregarde. We'll get her repaired if it's the last thing we do. I am sorry about it all, I really am . . .'

Already the ten Oompa-Loompas were rolling the enormous blueberry across the floor of the Inventing Room towards the door that led to the

chocolate river where the boat was waiting. Mr
and Mrs Beauregarde hurried after them. The rest
of the party, including little Charlie Bucket and
Grandpa Joe, stood absolutely still and watched
them go.

'Listen!' whispered Charlie. 'Listen, Grandpa!
The Oompa-Loompas in the boat outside are starting to sing!'

The voices, one hundred of them singing together, came loud and clear into the room:

'*Dear friends, we surely all agree*
There's almost nothing worse to see
Than some repulsive little bum
Who's always chewing chewing-gum.

(*It's very near as bad as those*
Who sit around and pick the nose.)
So please believe us when we say
That chewing gum will never pay;
This sticky habit's bound to send
The chewer to a sticky end.
Did any of you ever know
A person called Miss Bigelow?
This dreadful woman saw no wrong
In chewing, chewing all day long.
She chewed while bathing in the tub,
She chewed while dancing at her club,
She chewed in church and on the bus;
It really was quite ludicrous!
And when she couldn't find her gum,
She'd chew up the linoleum,
Or anything that happened near –
A pair of boots, the postman's ear,
Or other people's underclothes,
And once she chewed her boy-friend's nose.
She went on chewing till, at last,
Her chewing muscles grew so vast
That from her face her giant chin
Stuck out just like a violin.
For years and years she chewed away,
Consuming fifty bits a day,
Until one summer's eve, alas,
A horrid business came to pass.
Miss Bigelow went late to bed,
For half an hour she lay and read,
Chewing and chewing all the while
Like some great clockwork crocodile.

At last, she put her gum away
Upon a special little tray,
And settled back and went to sleep –
(She managed this by counting sheep).
But now, how strange! Although she slept,
Those massive jaws of hers still kept
On chewing, chewing through the night,
Even with nothing there to bite.
They were, you see, in such a groove
They positively had to move.
And very grim it was to hear
In pitchy darkness, loud and clear,
This sleeping woman's great big trap
Opening and shutting, snap-snap-snap!
Faster and faster, chop-chop-chop,
The noise went on, it wouldn't stop.
Until at last her jaws decide
To pause and open extra wide,
And with the most tremendous chew
They bit the lady's tongue in two.
Thereafter, just from chewing gum,
Miss Bigelow was always dumb,
And spent her life shut up in some
Disgusting sanatorium.
And that is why we'll try so hard
To save Miss Violet Beauregarde
From suffering an equal fate.
She's still quite young. It's not too late,
Provided she survives the cure.
We hope she does. We can't be sure.'

Along the Corridor

'Well, well, well,' sighed Mr Willy Wonka, 'two naughty little children gone. Three good little children left. I think we'd better get out of this room quickly before we lose anyone else!'

'But Mr Wonka,' said Charlie Bucket anxiously, 'will Violet Beauregarde *ever* be all right again or will she always be a blueberry?'

'They'll de-juice her in no time flat!' declared Mr Wonka. 'They'll roll her into the de-juicing machine, and she'll come out just as thin as a whistle!'

'But will she still be blue all over?' asked Charlie.

'She'll be *purple*!' cried Mr Wonka. 'A fine rich purple from head to toe! But there you are! That's what comes from chewing disgusting gum all day long!'

'If you think gum is so disgusting,' said Mike Teavee, 'then why do you make it in your factory?'

'I do wish you wouldn't mumble,' said Mr Wonka. 'I can't hear a word you're saying. Come on! Off we go! Hurry up! Follow me! We're going into the corridors again!' And so saying, Mr

Wonka scuttled across to the far end of the Inventing Room and went out through a small secret door hidden behind a lot of pipes and stoves. The three remaining children – Veruca Salt, Mike Teavee, and Charlie Bucket – together with the five remaining grown-ups, followed after him.

Charlie Bucket saw that they were now back in one of those long pink corridors with many other pink corridors leading out of it. Mr Wonka was rushing along in front, turning left and right and right and left, and Grandpa Joe was saying, 'Keep a good hold of my hand, Charlie. It would be terrible to get lost in here.'

Mr Wonka was saying, 'No time for any more

messing about! We'll never get *anywhere* at the rate we've been going!' And on he rushed, down the endless pink corridors, with his black top hat perched on the top of his head and his plum-coloured velvet coat-tails flying out behind him like a flag in the wind.

They passed a door in the wall. 'No time to go in!' shouted Mr Wonka. 'Press on! Press on!'

They passed another door, then another and another. There were doors every twenty paces or so along the corridor now, and they all had something written on them, and strange clanking noises were coming from behind several of them, and delicious smells came wafting through the keyholes, and sometimes little jets of coloured steam shot out from the cracks underneath.

Grandpa Joe and Charlie were half running and half walking to keep up with Mr Wonka, but they were able to read what it said on quite a few of the doors as they hurried by. EATABLE MARSHMALLOW PILLOWS, it said on one.

'Marshmallow pillows are terrific!' shouted Mr Wonka as he dashed by. 'They'll be all the rage when I get them into the shops! No time to go in, though! No time to go in!'

LICKABLE WALLPAPER FOR NUR-SERIES, it said on the next door.

'Lovely stuff, lickable wallpaper!' cried Mr Wonka, rushing past. 'It has pictures of fruits on it – bananas, apples, oranges, grapes, pineapples, strawberries, and snozzberries . . .'

'*Snozzberries?*' said Mike Teavee.

'Don't interrupt!' said Mr Wonka. 'The wallpaper has pictures of all these fruits printed on it, and when you lick the picture of a banana, it tastes of banana. When you lick a strawberry, it tastes of strawberry. And when you lick a snozzberry, it tastes just exactly like a snozzberry . . .'

'But what *does* a snozzberry taste like?'

'You're mumbling again,' said Mr Wonka. 'Speak louder next time. On we go! Hurry up!'

HOT ICE CREAMS FOR COLD DAYS, it said on the next door.

'*Extremely* useful in the winter,' said Mr Wonka, rushing on. 'Hot ice cream warms you up no end in freezing weather. I also make hot ice cubes for putting in hot drinks. Hot ice cubes make hot drinks hotter.'

COWS THAT GIVE CHOCOLATE MILK, it said on the next door.

'Ah, my pretty little cows!' cried Mr Wonka. 'How I love those cows!'

'But why can't we *see* them?' asked Veruca Salt. 'Why do we have to go rushing on past all these lovely rooms?'

'We shall stop in time!' called out Mr Wonka. 'Don't be so madly impatient!'

FIZZY LIFTING DRINKS, it said on the next door.

'Oh, those are fabulous!' cried Mr Wonka. 'They fill you with bubbles, and the bubbles are full of a special kind of gas, and this gas is so terrifically *lifting* that it lifts you right off the ground just like a balloon, and up you go until your head hits the ceiling – and there you stay.'

'But how do you come down again?' asked little Charlie.

'You do a burp, of course,' said Mr Wonka. 'You do a great big long rude burp, and *up* comes the gas and down comes you! But don't drink it outdoors! There's no knowing how high up you'll be carried if you do that. I gave some to an old Oompa-Loompa once out in the back yard and he went up and up and disappeared out of sight! It was very sad. I never saw him again.'

'He should have burped,' Charlie said.

'Of course he should have burped,' said Mr Wonka. 'I stood there shouting, "Burp, you silly ass, burp, or you'll never come down again!" But he didn't or couldn't or wouldn't, I don't know which. Maybe he was too polite. He must be on the moon by now.'

On the next door, it said, SQUARE SWEETS THAT LOOK ROUND.

'Wait!' cried Mr Wonka, skidding suddenly to a halt. 'I am very proud of my square sweets that look round. Let's take a peek.'

Square Sweets That Look Round

Everybody stopped and crowded to the door. The top half of the door was made of glass. Grandpa Joe lifted Charlie up so that he could get a better view, and looking in, Charlie saw a long table, and on the table there were rows and rows of small white square-shaped sweets. The sweets looked very much like square sugar lumps – except that each of them had a funny little pink face painted on one side. At the end of the table, a number of Oompa-Loompas were busily painting more faces on more sweets.

'There you are!' cried Mr Wonka. 'Square sweets that look round!'

'They don't look round to me,' said Mike Teavee.

'They look square,' said Veruca Salt. 'They look completely square.'

'But they *are* square,' said Mr Wonka. 'I never said they weren't.'

'You said they were *round*!' said Veruca Salt.

'I never said anything of the sort,' said Mr Wonka. 'I said they *looked* round.'

'But they *don't* look round!' said Veruca Salt.

'They look square!'

'They look round,' insisted Mr Wonka.

'They most certainly do not look round!' cried Veruca Salt.

'Veruca, darling,' said Mrs Salt, 'pay no attention to Mr Wonka! He's lying to you!'

'My dear old fish,' said Mr Wonka, 'go and boil your head!'

'How dare you speak to me like that!' shouted Mrs Salt.

'Oh, do shut up,' said Mr Wonka. 'Now watch this!'

He took a key from his pocket, and unlocked the door, and flung it open . . . and suddenly . . . at the sound of the door opening, all the rows of little square sweets looked quickly round to see who was

coming in. The tiny faces actually turned towards the door and stared at Mr Wonka.

'There you are!' he cried triumphantly. 'They're looking round! There's no argument about it! They are square sweets that look round!'

'By golly, he's right!' said Grandpa Joe.

'Come on!' said Mr Wonka, starting off down the corridor again. 'On we go! We mustn't dawdle!'

BUTTERSCOTCH AND BUTTERGIN, it said on the next door they passed.

'Now *that* sounds a bit more interesting,' said Mr Salt, Veruca's father.

'Glorious stuff!' said Mr Wonka. 'The Oompa-Loompas all adore it. It makes them tiddly. Listen! You can hear them in there now, whooping it up.'

Shrieks of laughter and snatches of singing could be heard coming through the closed door.

'They're drunk as lords,' said Mr Wonka. 'They're drinking butterscotch and soda. They like that best of all. Buttergin and tonic is also very popular. Follow me, please! We really mustn't keep stopping like this.' He turned left. He turned right. They came to a long flight of stairs. Mr Wonka slid down the banisters. The three children did the same. Mrs Salt and Mrs Teavee, the only women now left in the party, were getting very out of breath. Mrs Salt was a great fat creature with short legs, and she was blowing like a rhinoceros. 'This way!' cried Mr Wonka, turning left at the bottom of the stairs.

'Go *slower*!' panted Mrs Salt.

'Impossible,' said Mr Wonka. 'We should never get there in time if I did.'

'Get where?' asked Veruca Salt.

'Never you mind,' said Mr Wonka. 'You just wait and see.'

24

Veruca in the Nut Room

Mr Wonka rushed on down the corridor. THE NUT ROOM, it said on the next door they came to.

'All right,' said Mr Wonka, 'stop here for a moment and catch your breath, and take a peek through the glass panel of this door. But don't go in! Whatever you do, don't go into THE NUT ROOM! If you go in, you'll disturb the squirrels!'

Everyone crowded around the door.

'Oh look, Grandpa, look!' cried Charlie.

'Squirrels!' shouted Veruca Salt.

'Crikey!' said Mike Teavee.

It was an amazing sight. One hundred squirrels were seated upon high stools around a large table. On the table, there were mounds and mounds of walnuts, and the squirrels were all working away like mad, shelling the walnuts at a tremendous speed.

'These squirrels are specially trained for getting the nuts out of walnuts,' Mr Wonka explained.

'Why use squirrels?' Mike Teavee asked. 'Why not use Oompa-Loompas?'

'Because,' said Mr Wonka, 'Oompa-Loompas

can't get walnuts out of walnut shells in one piece. They always break them in two. Nobody except squirrels can get walnuts *whole* out of walnut shells every time. It is extremely difficult. But in my factory, I insist upon only whole walnuts. Therefore I have to have squirrels to do the job. Aren't they wonderful, the way they get those nuts out! And see how they first tap each walnut with their knuckles to be sure it's not a bad one! If it's bad, it makes a hollow sound, and they don't bother to open it. They just throw it down the rubbish chute. There! Look! Watch that squirrel nearest to us! I think he's got a bad one now!'

They watched the little squirrel as he tapped the walnut shell with his knuckles. He cocked his head to one side, listening intently, then suddenly he threw the nut over his shoulder into a large hole in the floor.

'Hey, Mummy!' shouted Veruca Salt suddenly,

'I've decided I want a squirrel! Get me one of those squirrels!'

'Don't be silly, sweetheart,' said Mrs Salt. 'These all belong to Mr Wonka.'

'I don't care about that!' shouted Veruca. 'I want one. All I've *got* at home is two dogs and four cats and six bunny rabbits and two parakeets and three canaries and a green parrot and a turtle and a bowl of goldfish and a cage of white mice and a silly old hamster! I want a *squirrel*!'

'All right, my pet,' Mrs Salt said soothingly. 'Mummy'll get you a squirrel just as soon as she possibly can.'

'But I don't want *any* old squirrel!' Veruca shouted. 'I want a *trained* squirrel!'

At this point, Mr Salt, Veruca's father, stepped forward. 'Very well, Wonka,' he said importantly, taking out a wallet full of money, 'how much d'you want for one of these squirrels? Name your price.'

'They're not for sale,' Mr Wonka answered. 'She can't have one.'

'Who says I can't!' shouted Veruca. 'I'm going in to get myself one this very minute!'

'Don't!' said Mr Wonka quickly, but he was too late. The girl had already thrown open the door and rushed in.

The moment she entered the room, one hundred squirrels stopped what they were doing and turned their heads and stared at her with small black beady eyes.

Veruca Salt stopped also, and stared back at them. Then her gaze fell upon a pretty little squirrel sitting nearest to her at the end of the table. The squirrel was holding a walnut in its paws.

'All right,' Veruca said, 'I'll have *you*!'

She reached out her hands to grab the squirrel ... but as she did so ... in that first split second when her hands started to go forward, there was a sudden flash of movement in the room, like a flash of brown lightning, and every single squirrel around the table took a flying leap towards her and landed on her body.

Twenty-five of them caught hold of her right arm, and pinned it down.

Twenty-five more caught hold of her left arm, and pinned that down.

Twenty-five caught hold of her right leg and anchored it to the ground.

Twenty-*four* caught hold of her left leg.

And the one remaining squirrel (obviously the leader of them all) climbed up on to her shoulder and started tap-tap-tapping the wretched girl's head with its knuckles.

'Save her!' screamed Mrs Salt. 'Veruca! Come back! What are they *doing* to her?'

'They're testing her to see if she's a bad nut,' said Mr Wonka. 'You watch.'

Veruca struggled furiously, but the squirrels held her tight and she couldn't move. The squirrel on her shoulder went tap-tap-tapping the side of her head with his knuckles.

Then all at once, the squirrels pulled Veruca to the ground and started carrying her across the floor.

'My goodness, she *is* a bad nut after all,' said Mr Wonka. 'Her head must have sounded quite hollow.'

Veruca kicked and screamed, but it was no use. The tiny strong paws held her tightly and she couldn't escape.

'Where are they taking her?' shrieked Mrs Salt.

'She's going where all the other bad nuts go,' said Mr Willy Wonka. 'Down the rubbish chute.'

'By golly, she *is* going down the chute!' said Mr Salt, staring through the glass door at his daughter.

'Then save her!' cried Mrs Salt.

'Too late,' said Mr Wonka. 'She's gone!'

And indeed she had.

'But where?' shrieked Mrs Salt, flapping her arms. 'What happens to the bad nuts? Where does the chute go to?'

'That *particular* chute,' Mr Wonka told her, 'runs directly into the great big main rubbish pipe which carries away all the rubbish from every part of the factory – all the floor sweepings and potato peelings and rotten cabbages and fish heads and stuff like that.'

'Who eats fish and cabbage and potatoes in *this* factory, I'd like to know?' said Mike Teavee.

'I do, of course,' answered Mr Wonka. 'You don't think I live on cacao beans, do you?'

'But ... but ... but ...' shrieked Mrs Salt, 'where does the great big pipe go to in the end?'

'Why, to the furnace, of course,' Mr Wonka said calmly. 'To the incinerator.'

Mrs Salt opened her huge red mouth and started to scream.

'Don't worry,' said Mr Wonka, 'there's always a chance that they've decided not to light it today.'

'A *chance*!' yelled Mrs Salt. 'My darling Veruca! She'll . . . she'll . . . she'll be sizzled like a sausage!'

'Quite right, my dear,' said Mr Salt. 'Now see here, Wonka,' he added, 'I think you've gone *just* a shade too far this time, I do indeed. My daughter may be a bit of a frump – I don't mind admitting it – but that doesn't mean you can roast her to a crisp. I'll have you know I'm extremely cross about this, I really am.'

'Oh, don't be cross, my dear sir!' said Mr Wonka. 'I expect she'll turn up again sooner or later. She may not even have gone down at all. She may be stuck in the chute just below the entrance hole, and if *that's* the case, all you'll have to do is go in and pull her up again.'

Hearing this, both Mr and Mrs Salt dashed into the Nut Room and ran over to the hole in the floor and peered in.

'Veruca!' shouted Mrs Salt. 'Are you down there!'

There was no answer.

Mrs Salt bent further forward to get a closer look. She was now kneeling right on the edge of the hole with her head down and her enormous behind sticking up in the air like a giant mushroom. It was a dangerous position to be in. She needed only one tiny little push ... one gentle nudge in the right place ... and *that* is exactly what the squirrels gave her! Over she toppled, into the hole head first, screeching like a parrot.

'Good gracious me!' said Mr Salt, as he watched his fat wife go tumbling down the hole, 'what a lot of rubbish there's going to be today!' He saw her disappearing into the darkness. 'What's it like down

there, Angina?' he called out. He leaned further forward.

The squirrels rushed up behind him . . .

'Help!' he shouted.

But he was already toppling forward, and down the chute he went, just as his wife had done before him – and his daughter.

'Oh *dear*!' cried Charlie, who was watching with the others through the door, 'what on earth's going to happen to them now?'

'I expect someone will catch them at the bottom of the chute,' said Mr Wonka.

'But what about the great fiery incinerator?' asked Charlie.

'They only light it every other day,' said Mr Wonka. 'Perhaps this is one of the days when they let it go out. You never know . . . they might be lucky . . .'

'Ssshh!' said Grandpa Joe. 'Listen! Here comes another song!'

From far away down the corridor came the beating of drums. Then the singing began.

> *'Veruca Salt!'* sang the Oompa-Loompas.
> *'Veruca Salt, the little brute,*
> *Has just gone down the rubbish chute*
> *(And as we very rightly thought*
> *That in a case like this we ought*
> *To see the thing completely through,*
> *We've polished off her parents, too).*
> *Down goes Veruca! Down the drain!*
> *And here, perhaps, we should explain*
> *That she will meet, as she descends,*
> *A rather different set of friends*
> *To those that she has left behind –*
> *These won't be nearly so refined.*
> *A fish head, for example, cut*
> *This morning from a halibut.*
> *"Hello! Good morning! How d'you do?*
> *How nice to meet you! How are you?"*
> *And then a little further down*
> *A mass of others gather round:*
> *A bacon rind, some rancid lard,*
> *A loaf of bread gone stale and hard,*
> *A steak that nobody could chew,*
> *An oyster from an oyster stew,*

Some liverwurst so old and grey
One smelled it from a mile away,
A rotten nut, a reeky pear,
A thing the cat left on the stair,
And lots of other things as well,
Each with a rather horrid smell.
These are Veruca's new-found friends
That she will meet as she descends,
And this is the price she has to pay
For going so very far astray.
But now, my dears, we think you might
Be wondering — is it really right
That every single bit of blame
And all the scolding and the shame
Should fall upon Veruca Salt?
Is she the only one at fault?
For though she's spoiled, and dreadfully so,
A girl can't spoil herself, you know.
Who spoiled her, then? Ah, who indeed?
Who pandered to her every need?
Who turned her into such a brat?
Who are the culprits? Who did that?
Alas! You needn't look so far
To find out who these sinners are.
They are (and this is very sad)
Her loving parents, MUM and DAD.
And that is why we're glad they fell
Into the rubbish chute as well.'

The Great Glass Lift

'I've never seen anything like it!' cried Mr Wonka. 'The children are disappearing like rabbits! But you mustn't worry about it! They'll *all* come out in the wash!'

Mr Wonka looked at the little group that stood beside him in the corridor. There were only two children left now – Mike Teavee and Charlie Bucket. And there were three grown-ups, Mr and Mrs Teavee and Grandpa Joe. 'Shall we move on?' Mr Wonka asked.

'Oh, yes!' cried Charlie and Grandpa Joe, both together.

'My feet are getting tired,' said Mike Teavee. 'I want to watch television.'

'If you're tired then we'd better take the lift,' said Mr Wonka. 'It's over here. Come on! In we go!' He skipped across the passage to a pair of double doors. The doors slid open. The two children and the grown-ups went in.

'Now then,' cried Mr Wonka, 'which button shall we press first? Take your pick!'

Charlie Bucket stared around him in astonishment. This was the craziest lift he had ever seen.

There were buttons everywhere! The walls, and even the *ceiling,* were covered all over with rows and rows and rows of small, black push buttons! There must have been a thousand of them on each wall, and another thousand on the ceiling! And now Charlie noticed that every single button had a tiny printed label beside it telling you which room you would be taken to if you pressed it.

'This isn't just an ordinary up-and-down lift!' announced Mr Wonka proudly. 'This lift can go sideways and longways and slantways and any other way you can think of! It can visit any single room in the whole factory, no matter where it is! You simply press the button . . . and *zing!* . . . you're off!'

'*Fantastic!*' murmured Grandpa Joe. His eyes were shining with excitement as he stared at the rows of buttons.

'The whole lift is made of thick, clear glass!' Mr Wonka declared. 'Walls, doors, ceiling, floor, everything is made of glass so that you can see out!'

'But there's nothing to see,' said Mike Teavee.

'Choose a button!' said Mr Wonka. 'The two children may press one button each. So take your pick! Hurry up! In every room, something delicious and wonderful is being made.'

Quickly, Charlie started reading some of the labels alongside the buttons.

THE ROCK-CANDY MINE – 10,000 FEET DEEP, it said on one.

COKERNUT-ICE SKATING RINKS, it said on another.

Then ... STRAWBERRY-JUICE WATER PISTOLS.

TOFFEE-APPLE TREES FOR PLANTING OUT IN YOUR GARDEN – ALL SIZES.

EXPLODING SWEETS FOR YOUR ENEMIES.

LUMINOUS LOLLIES FOR EATING IN BED AT NIGHT.

MINT JUJUBES FOR THE BOY NEXT DOOR – THEY'LL GIVE HIM GREEN TEETH FOR A MONTH.

CAVITY-FILLING CARAMELS – NO MORE DENTISTS.

STICKJAW FOR TALKATIVE PARENTS.

WRIGGLE-SWEETS THAT WRIGGLE DELIGHTFULLY IN YOUR TUMMY AFTER SWALLOWING.

INVISIBLE CHOCOLATE BARS FOR EATING IN CLASS.

SUGAR-COATED PENCILS FOR SUCKING.

FIZZY LEMONADE SWIMMING POOLS.

MAGIC HAND-FUDGE – WHEN YOU HOLD IT IN YOUR HAND, YOU TASTE IT IN YOUR MOUTH.

RAINBOW DROPS – SUCK THEM AND YOU CAN SPIT IN SIX DIFFERENT COLOURS.

'Come on, come on!' cried Mr Wonka. 'We can't wait all day!'

'Isn't there a *Television Room* in all this lot?' asked Mike Teavee.

'Certainly there's a television room,' Mr Wonka said. 'That button over there.' He pointed with his finger. Everybody looked. TELEVISION CHOCOLATE, it said on the tiny label beside the button.

'*Whoopee!*' shouted Mike Teavee. 'That's for me!' He stuck out his thumb and pressed the button. Instantly, there was a tremendous whizzing noise. The doors clanged shut and the lift leaped away as though it had been stung by a wasp. But it leapt *sideways*! And all the passengers (except Mr Wonka, who was holding on to a strap from the ceiling) were flung off their feet on to the floor.

'Get up, get up!' cried Mr Wonka, roaring with laughter. But just as they were staggering to their feet, the lift changed direction and swerved violently round a corner. And over they went once more.

'Help!' shouted Mrs Teavee.

'Take my hand, madam,' said Mr Wonka gallantly. 'There you are! Now grab this strap! Everybody grab a strap. The journey's not over yet!'

Old Grandpa Joe staggered to his feet and caught hold of a strap. Little Charlie, who couldn't possibly reach as high as that, put his arms around Grandpa Joe's legs and hung on tight.

The lift rushed on at the speed of a rocket. Now it was beginning to climb. It was shooting up and

up and up on a steep slanty course as if it were climbing a very steep hill. Then suddenly, as though it had come to the top of the hill and gone over a precipice, it dropped like a stone and Charlie felt his tummy coming right up into his throat, and

Grandpa Joe shouted, 'Yippee! Here we go!' and Mrs Teavee cried out, 'The rope has broken! We're going to crash!' And Mr Wonka said, 'Calm yourself, my dear lady,' and patted her comfortingly on the arm. And then Grandpa Joe looked down at Charlie who was clinging to his legs, and he said, 'Are you all right, Charlie?' Charlie shouted, 'I love it! It's like being on a roller coaster!' And through the glass walls of the lift, as it rushed along, they caught sudden glimpses of strange and wonderful things going on in some of the other rooms:

An enormous spout with brown sticky stuff oozing out of it on to the floor . . .

A great, craggy mountain made entirely of fudge, with Oompa-Loompas (all roped together for safety) hacking huge hunks of fudge out of its sides . . .

A machine with white powder spraying out of it like a snowstorm . . .

A lake of hot caramel with steam coming off it . . .

A village of Oompa-Loompas, with tiny houses and streets and hundreds of Oompa-Loompa children no more than four inches high playing in the streets . . .

And now the lift began flattening out again, but it seemed to be going faster than ever, and Charlie could hear the scream of the wind outside as it hurtled forward . . . and it twisted . . . and it turned . . . and it went up . . . and it went down . . . and . . .

'I'm going to be sick!' yelled Mrs Teavee, turning green in the face.

'Please don't be sick,' said Mr Wonka.

'Try and stop me!' said Mrs Teavee.

'Then you'd better take this,' said Mr Wonka, and he swept his magnificent black top hat off his head, and held it out, upside down, in front of Mrs Teavee's mouth.

'Make this awful thing stop!' ordered Mr Teavee.

'Can't do that,' said Mr Wonka. 'It won't stop till we get there. I only hope no one's using the *other* lift at this moment.'

'What other lift?' screamed Mrs Teavee.

'The one that goes the opposite way on the same track as this one,' said Mr Wonka.

'Holy mackerel!' cried Mr Teavee. 'You mean we might have a collision?'

'I've always been lucky so far,' said Mr Wonka.

'Now I *am* going to be sick!' yelled Mrs Teavee.

'No, no!' said Mr Wonka. 'Not now! We're nearly there! Don't spoil my hat!'

The next moment, there was a screaming of brakes, and the lift began to slow down. Then it stopped altogether.

'Some ride!' said Mr Teavee, wiping his great sweaty face with a handkerchief.

'Never again!' gasped Mrs Teavee. And then the doors of the lift slid open and Mr Wonka said, 'Just a minute now! Listen to me! I want everybody to be very careful in this room. There is dangerous stuff around in here and you *must not* tamper with it.'

The Television-Chocolate Room

The Teavee family, together with Charlie and Grandpa Joe, stepped out of the lift into a room so dazzlingly bright and dazzlingly white that they screwed up their eyes in pain and stopped walking. Mr Wonka handed each of them a pair of dark glasses and said, 'Put these on quick! And don't take them off in here whatever you do! This light could blind you!'

As soon as Charlie had his dark glasses on, he was able to look around him in comfort. He saw a long narrow room. The room was painted white all over. Even the floor was white, and there wasn't a speck of dust anywhere. From the ceiling, huge lamps hung down and bathed the room in a brilliant blue-white light. The room was completely bare except at the far ends. At one of these ends there was an enormous camera on wheels, and a whole army of Oompa-Loompas was clustering around it, oiling its joints and adjusting its knobs and polishing its great glass lens. The Oompa-Loompas were all dressed in the most extraordinary way. They were wearing bright-red space suits, complete with helmets and goggles – at least they looked like space suits – and they were working in complete silence. Watching them, Charlie experienced a queer sense of danger. There was something dangerous about this whole business, and the Oompa-Loompas knew it. There was no chattering or singing among them here, and they moved about over the huge black camera slowly and carefully in their scarlet space suits.

At the other end of the room, about fifty paces away from the camera, a single Oompa-Loompa (also wearing a space suit) was sitting at a black table gazing at the screen of a very large television set.

'Here we go!' cried Mr Wonka, hopping up and down with excitement. 'This is the Testing Room for my very latest and greatest invention – Television Chocolate!'

'But what *is* Television Chocolate?' asked Mike Teavee.

'Good heavens, child, stop interrupting me!' said Mr Wonka. 'It works by television. I don't like television myself. I suppose it's all right in small doses, but children never seem to be able to take it in small doses. They want to sit there all day long staring and staring at the screen . . .'

'That's me!' said Mike Teavee.

'Shut up!' said Mr Teavee.

'Thank you,' said Mr Wonka. 'I shall now tell you how this amazing television set of mine works. But first of all, do you know how ordinary television works? It is very simple. At one end, where the picture is being taken, you have a large ciné camera and you start photographing something. The photographs are then split up into millions of tiny little pieces which are so small that you can't see them, and these little pieces are shot out into the sky by electricity. In the sky, they go whizzing around all over the place until suddenly they hit the antenna on the roof of somebody's house. They then go flashing down the wire that leads right into the back of the television set, and in there they get jiggled and joggled around until at last every single one of those millions of tiny pieces is fitted back into its right place (just like a jigsaw puzzle), and presto! – the photograph appears on the screen . . .'

'That isn't *exactly* how it works,' Mike Teavee said.

'I am a little deaf in my left ear,' Mr Wonka said. 'You must forgive me if I don't hear everything you say.'

'I said, that isn't *exactly* how it works!' shouted Mike Teavee.

'You're a nice boy,' Mr Wonka said, 'but you talk too much. Now then! The very first time I saw ordinary television working, I was struck by a tremendous idea. "Look here!" I shouted. "If these people can break up a *photograph* into millions of pieces and send the pieces whizzing through the air and then put them together again at the other end, why can't I do the same thing with a bar of chocolate? Why can't *I* send a real bar of chocolate whizzing through the air in tiny pieces and then put the pieces together at the other end, all ready to be eaten?"'

'Impossible!' said Mike Teavee.

'You think so?' cried Mr Wonka. 'Well, watch this! I shall now send a bar of my very best chocolate from one end of this room to the other – by television! Get ready, there! Bring in the chocolate!'

Immediately, six Oompa-Loompas marched forward carrying on their shoulders the most enormous bar of chocolate Charlie had ever seen. It was about the size of the mattress he slept on at home.

'It has to be big,' Mr Wonka explained, 'because whenever you send something by television, it always comes out much smaller than it was when it went in. Even with *ordinary* television, when you photograph a big man, he never comes out on your screen any taller than a pencil, does he? Here we go, then! Get ready! *No, no! Stop! Hold everything!* You there! Mike Teavee! Stand back! You're too close to the camera! There are dangerous rays coming out of that thing! They could break you up into a million tiny pieces in one second! That's why the Oompa-Loompas are wearing space suits! The suits protect them! All right! That's better! Now, then! *Switch on!*'

One of the Oompa-Loompas caught hold of a large switch and pulled it down.

There was a blinding flash.

'The chocolate's gone!' shouted Grandpa Joe, waving his arms.

He was quite right! The whole enormous bar of chocolate had disappeared completely into thin air!

'It's on its way!' cried Mr Wonka. 'It is now rushing through the air above our heads in a million tiny pieces. Quick! Come over here!' He dashed over to the other end of the room where the large television set was standing, and the others followed him. 'Watch the screen!' he cried. 'Here it comes! Look!'

The screen flickered and lit up. Then suddenly, a small bar of chocolate appeared in the middle of the screen.

158

'Take it!' shouted Mr Wonka, growing more and more excited.

'How can you take it?' asked Mike Teavee, laughing. 'It's just a picture on a television screen!'

'Charlie Bucket!' cried Mr Wonka. '*You* take it! Reach out and grab it!'

Charlie put out his hand and touched the screen, and suddenly, miraculously, the bar of chocolate came away in his fingers. He was so surprised he nearly dropped it.

'Eat it!' shouted Mr Wonka. 'Go on and eat it! It'll be delicious! It's the same bar! It's got smaller on the journey, that's all!'

'It's absolutely fantastic!' gasped Grandpa Joe. 'It's . . . it's . . . it's a miracle!'

'Just imagine,' cried Mr Wonka, 'when I start using this across the country . . . you'll be sitting at home watching television and suddenly a commercial will flash on to the screen and a voice will say, "EAT WONKA'S CHOCOLATES! THEY'RE THE BEST IN THE WORLD! IF YOU DON'T BELIEVE US, TRY ONE FOR YOURSELF – *NOW*!" And you simply reach out and take one! How about that, eh?'

'Terrific!' cried Grandpa Joe. 'It will change the world!'

Mike Teavee is Sent by Television

Mike Teavee was even more excited than Grandpa Joe at seeing a bar of chocolate being sent by television. 'But Mr Wonka,' he shouted, 'can you send *other things* through the air in the same way? Breakfast cereal, for instance?'

'Oh, my sainted aunt!' cried Mr Wonka. 'Don't mention that disgusting stuff in front of me! Do you know what breakfast cereal is made of? It's made of all those little curly wooden shavings you find in pencil sharpeners!'

'But could you send it by television if you wanted to, as you do chocolate?' asked Mike Teavee.

'Of course I could!'

'And what about people?' asked Mike Teavee. 'Could you send a real live person from one place to another in the same way?'

'A *person!*' cried Mr Wonka. 'Are you off your rocker?'

'But *could* it be done?'

'Good heavens, child, I really don't know . . . I suppose it *could* . . . yes. I'm pretty sure it could . . . of course it could . . . I wouldn't like to risk it, though . . . it might have some very nasty results . . .'

But Mike Teavee was already off and running. The moment he heard Mr Wonka saying, 'I'm pretty sure it could . . . of course it could,' he turned away and started running as fast as he could towards the other end of the room where the great camera was standing. 'Look at me!' he shouted as he ran. 'I'm going to be the first person in the world to be sent by television!'

'*No, no, no, no!*' cried Mr Wonka.

'Mike!' screamed Mrs Teavee. 'Stop! Come back! You'll be turned into a million tiny pieces!'

But there was no stopping Mike Teavee now. The crazy boy rushed on, and when he reached the enormous camera, he jumped straight for the switch, scattering Oompa-Loompas right and left as he went.

'See you later, alligator!' he shouted, and he pulled down the switch, and as he did so, he leaped out into the full glare of the mighty lens.

There was a blinding flash.

Then there was silence.

Then Mrs Teavee ran forward . . . but she stopped dead in the middle of the room . . . and she stood there . . . she stood staring at the place where her son had been . . . and her great red mouth opened wide and she screamed, 'He's gone! He's gone!'

'Great heavens, he *has* gone!' shouted Mr Teavee.

Mr Wonka hurried forward and placed a hand

gently on Mrs Teavee's shoulder. 'We shall have to hope for the best,' he said. 'We must pray that your little boy will come out unharmed at the other end.'

'Mike!' screamed Mrs Teavee, clasping her head in her hands. 'Where are you?'

'I'll tell you where he is,' said Mr Teavee, 'he's whizzing around above our heads in a million tiny pieces!'

'Don't talk about it!' wailed Mrs Teavee.

'We must watch the television set,' said Mr Wonka. 'He may come through any moment.'

Mr and Mrs Teavee and Grandpa Joe and little Charlie and Mr Wonka all gathered round the television and stared tensely at the screen. The screen was quite blank.

'He's taking a heck of a long time to come across,' said Mr Teavee, wiping his brow.

'Oh dear, oh dear,' said Mr Wonka, 'I do hope that no part of him gets left behind.'

'What on earth do you mean?' asked Mr Teavee sharply.

'I don't wish to alarm you,' said Mr Wonka, 'but it does sometimes happen that only about half the little pieces find their way into the television set. It happened last week. I don't know why, but the result was that only half a bar of chocolate came through.'

Mrs Teavee let out a scream of horror. 'You mean only a half of Mike is coming back to us?' she cried.

'Let's hope it's the top half,' said Mr Teavee.

'Hold everything!' said Mr Wonka. 'Watch the screen! Something's happening!'

The screen had suddenly begun to flicker.

Then some wavy lines appeared.

Mr Wonka adjusted one of the knobs and the wavy lines went away.

And now, very slowly, the screen began to get brighter and brighter.

'Here he comes!' yelled Mr Wonka. 'Yes, that's him all right!'

'Is he all in one piece?' cried Mrs Teavee.

'I'm not sure,' said Mr Wonka. 'It's too early to tell.'

Faintly at first, but becoming clearer and clearer every second, the picture of Mike Teavee appeared on the screen. He was standing up and waving at the audience and grinning from ear to ear.

'But he's a midget!' shouted Mr Teavee.

'Mike,' cried Mrs Teavee, 'are you all right? Are there any bits of you missing?'

'Isn't he going to get any bigger?' shouted Mr Teavee.

'Talk to me, Mike!' cried Mrs Teavee. 'Say something! Tell me you're all right!'

A tiny little voice, no louder than the squeaking of a mouse, came out of the television set. 'Hi, Mum!' it said. 'Hi, Pop! Look at *me*! I'm the first person ever to be sent by television!'

'Grab him!' ordered Mr Wonka. 'Quick!'

Mrs Teavee shot out a hand and picked the tiny figure of Mike Teavee out of the screen.

'Hooray!' cried Mr Wonka. 'He's all in one piece! He's completely unharmed!'

'You call *that* unharmed?' snapped Mrs Teavee, peering at the little speck of a boy who was now running to and fro across the palm of her hand, waving his pistols in the air.

He was certainly not more than an inch tall.

'He's *shrunk*!' said Mr Teavee.

'Of course he's shrunk,' said Mr Wonka. 'What did you expect?'

'This is terrible!' wailed Mrs Teavee. 'What *are* we going to do?'

And Mr Teavee said, 'We can't send him back

to school like this! He'll get trodden on! He'll get squashed!'

'He won't be able to do *anything*!' cried Mrs Teavee.

'Oh, yes I will!' squeaked the tiny voice of Mike Teavee. 'I'll still be able to watch television!'

'*Never again*!' shouted Mr Teavee. 'I'm throwing the television set right out the window the moment we get home. I've had enough of television!'

When he heard this, Mike Teavee flew into a terrible tantrum. He started jumping up and down on the palm of his mother's hand, screaming and yelling and trying to bite her fingers. 'I want to watch television!' he squeaked. 'I want to watch television! I want to watch television! I want to watch television!'

'Here! Give him to me!' said Mr Teavee, and he took the tiny boy and shoved him into thc breast pocket of his jacket and stuffed a handkerchief on top. Squeals and yells came from inside the pocket, and the pocket shook as the furious little prisoner fought to get out.

'Oh, Mr Wonka,' wailed Mrs Teavee, 'how can we make him grow?'

'Well,' said Mr Wonka, stroking his beard and gazing thoughtfully at the ceiling, 'I must say that's a wee bit tricky. But small boys are extremely springy and elastic. They stretch like mad. So what we'll do, we'll put him in a special machine I have for testing the stretchiness of chewing-gum! Maybe that will bring him back to what he was.'

'Oh, thank you!' said Mrs Teavee.

'Don't mention it, dear lady.'

'How far d'you think he'll stretch?' asked Mr Teavee.

'Maybe miles,' said Mr Wonka. 'Who knows? But he's going to be awfully thin. Everything gets thinner when you stretch it.'

'You mean like chewing-gum?' asked Mr Teavee.

'Exactly.'

'How thin will he be?' asked Mrs Teavee anxiously.

'I haven't the foggiest idea,' said Mr Wonka. 'And it doesn't really matter, anyway, because we'll soon fatten him up again. All we'll have to do is give him a triple overdose of my wonderful Supervitamin Chocolate. Supervitamin Chocolate contains huge amounts of vitamin A and vitamin B. It also contains vitamin C, vitamin D, vitamin E, vitamin F, vitamin G, vitamin I, vitamin J, vitamin K, vitamin L, vitamin M, vitamin N, vitamin O, vitamin P, vitamin Q, vitamin R, vitamin T, vitamin U, vitamin V, vitamin W, vitamin X, vitamin Y, *and*, believe it or not, vitamin Z! The only two vitamins it doesn't have in it are vitamin S, because it makes you sick, and vitamin H, because it makes you grow horns on the top of your head, like a bull. But it *does* have in it a very small amount of the rarest and most magical vitamin of them all – vitamin Wonka.'

'And what will *that* do to him?' asked Mr Teavee anxiously.

'It'll make his toes grow out until they're as long as his fingers . . .'

'Oh, no!' cried Mrs Teavee.

'Don't be silly,' said Mr Wonka. 'It's most useful. He'll be able to play the piano with his feet.'

'But Mr Wonka . . .'

'No arguments, *please*!' said Mr Wonka. He turned away and clicked his fingers three times in the air. An Oompa-Loompa appeared immediately and stood beside him. 'Follow these orders,' said

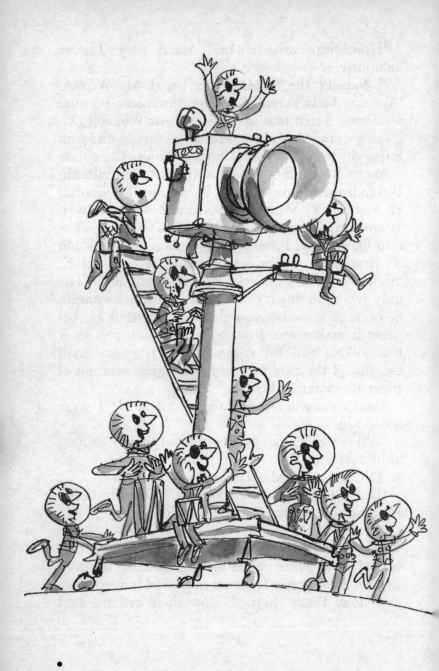

Mr Wonka, handing the Oompa-Loompa a piece of paper on which he had written full instructions. 'And you'll find the boy in his father's pocket. Off you go! Good-bye, Mr Teavee! Good-bye, Mrs Teavee! And please don't look so worried! They all come out in the wash, you know; every one of them . . .'

At the end of the room, the Oompa-Loompas around the giant camera were already beating their tiny drums and beginning to jog up and down to the rhythm.

'There they go again!' said Mr Wonka. 'I'm afraid you can't stop them singing.'

Little Charlie caught Grandpa Joe's hand, and the two of them stood beside Mr Wonka in the middle of the long bright room, listening to the Oompa-Loompas. And this is what they sang:

> '*The most important thing we've learned,*
> *So far as children are concerned,*
> *Is never, NEVER, NEVER let*
> *Them near your television set –*
> *Or better still, just don't install*
> *The idiotic thing at all.*
> *In almost every house we've been,*
> *We've watched them gaping at the screen.*
> *They loll and slop and lounge about,*
> *And stare until their eyes pop out.*
> *(Last week in someone's place we saw*
> *A dozen eyeballs on the floor.)*
> *They sit and stare and stare and sit*
> *Until they're hypnotized by it,*

Until they're absolutely drunk
With all that shocking ghastly junk.
Oh yes, we know it keeps them still,
They don't climb out the window sill,
They never fight or kick or punch,
They leave you free to cook the lunch
And wash the dishes in the sink —
But did you ever stop to think,
To wonder just exactly what
This does to your beloved tot?
IT ROTS THE SENSES IN THE HEAD!
IT KILLS IMAGINATION DEAD!
IT CLOGS AND CLUTTERS UP THE
   MIND!
IT MAKES A CHILD SO DULL AND BLIND
HE CAN NO LONGER UNDERSTAND
A FANTASY, A FAIRYLAND!
HIS BRAIN BECOMES AS SOFT AS
   CHEESE!
HIS POWERS OF THINKING RUST AND
   FREEZE!
HE CANNOT THINK – HE ONLY SEES!
"All right!" you'll cry. "All right!" you'll say,
"But if we take the set away,
What shall we do to entertain
Our darling children! Please explain!"
We'll answer this by asking you,
"What used the darling ones to do?
How used they keep themselves contented
Before this monster was invented?"
Have you forgotten? Don't you know?
We'll say it very loud and slow:

THEY ... USED ... TO ... READ! *They'd*
  READ and READ,
AND READ and *READ, and then proceed*
TO READ some more. Great Scott! Gadzooks!
One half their lives was reading books!
The nursery shelves held books galore!
Books cluttered up the nursery floor!
And in the bedroom, by the bed,
More books were waiting to be read!
Such wondrous, fine, fantastic tales
Of dragons, gypsies, queens, and whales
And treasure isles, and distant shores
Where smugglers rowed with muffled oars,
And pirates wearing purple pants,
And sailing ships and elephants,
And cannibals crouching round the pot,
Stirring away at something hot.
(It smells so good, what can it be?
Good gracious, it's Penelope.)
The younger ones had Beatrix Potter
With Mr Tod, the dirty rotter,
And Squirrel Nutkin, Pigling Bland,
And Mrs Tiggy-Winkle and –
Just How The Camel Got His Hump,
And How The Monkey Lost His Rump,
And Mr Toad, and bless my soul,
There's Mr Rat and Mr Mole –
Oh, books, what books they used to know,
Those children living long ago!
So please, oh please, *we beg, we pray,*
Go throw your TV set away,
And in its place you can install

A lovely bookshelf on the wall.
Then fill the shelves with lots of books,
Ignoring all the dirty looks,
The screams and yells, the bites and kicks,
And children hitting you with sticks —
Fear not, because we promise you
That, in about a week or two
Of having nothing else to do,
They'll now begin to feel the need
Of having something good to read.
And once they start — oh boy, oh boy!
You watch the slowly growing joy
That fills their hearts. They'll grow so keen
They'll wonder what they'd ever seen
In that ridiculous machine,
That nauseating, foul, unclean.
Repulsive television screen!
And later, each and every kid
Will love you more for what you did.
P.S. Regarding Mike Teavee,
We very much regret that we
Shall simply have to wait and see
If we can get him back his height.
But if we can't — it serves him right.'

28

Only Charlie Left

'Which room shall it be next?' said Mr Wonka as he turned away and darted into the lift. 'Come on! Hurry up! We *must* get going! And how many children are there left now?'

Little Charlie looked at Grandpa Joe, and Grandpa Joe looked back at little Charlie.

'But Mr Wonka,' Grandpa Joe called after him, 'there's . . . there's only Charlie left now.'

Mr Wonka swung round and stared at Charlie.

There was a silence. Charlie stood there holding tightly on to Grandpa Joe's hand.

'You mean you're the *only* one left?' Mr Wonka said, pretending to be surprised.

'Why, yes,' whispered Charlie. 'Yes.'

Mr Wonka suddenly exploded with excitement. 'But my *dear boy,*' he cried out, '*that means you've won*!' He rushed out of the lift and started shaking Charlie's hand so furiously it nearly came off. 'Oh, I do congratulate you!' he cried. 'I really do! I'm absolutely delighted! It couldn't be better! How wonderful this is! I had a hunch, you know, right from the beginning, that it was going to be you! Well *done*, Charlie, well *done*! This is terrific! Now

the fun is really going to start! But we mustn't
dilly! We mustn't dally! There's even less time to
lose now than there was before! We have an *enormous* number of things to do before the day is out!
Just think of the *arrangements* that have to be made!
And the people we have to fetch! But luckily for us,

we have the great glass lift to speed things up! Jump in, my dear Charlie, jump in! You too, Grandpa Joe, sir! No, no, *after* you! That's the way! Now then! This time *I* shall choose the button we are going to press!' Mr Wonka's bright twinkling blue eyes rested for a moment on Charlie's face.

Something crazy is going to happen now, Charlie thought. But he wasn't frightened. He wasn't even nervous. He was just terrifically excited. And so was Grandpa Joe. The old man's face was shining with excitement as he watched every move that Mr Wonka made. Mr Wonka was reaching for a button high up on the glass ceiling of the lift. Charlie and Grandpa Joe both craned their necks to read what it said on the little label beside the button.

It said . . . UP AND OUT.

'*Up* and *out*,' thought Charlie. 'What sort of a room is that?'

Mr Wonka pressed the button.

The glass doors closed.

'Hold on!' cried Mr Wonka.

Then *WHAM!* The lift shot straight up like a rocket! 'Yippee!' shouted Grandpa Joe. Charlie was clinging to Grandpa Joe's legs and Mr Wonka was holding on to a strap from the ceiling, and up they went, up, up, up, straight up this time, with no twistings or turnings, and Charlie could hear the whistling of the air outside as the lift went faster and faster. 'Yippee!' shouted Grandpa Joe again. 'Yippee! Here we go!'

'Faster!' cried Mr Wonka, banging the wall of the lift with his hand. 'Faster! Faster! If we don't go any faster than this, we shall never get through!'

'Through what?' shouted Grandpa Joe. 'What have we got to get through?'

'Ah-ha!' cried Mr Wonka, 'you wait and see! I've been *longing* to press this button for years! But I've never done it until now! I was tempted many times! Oh, yes, I was tempted! But I couldn't bear the thought of making a great big hole in the roof of the factory! Here we go, boys! Up and out!'

'But you don't mean . . .' shouted Grandpa Joe, '. . . you don't *really* mean that this lift . . .'

'Oh yes, I do!' answered Mr Wonka. 'You wait and see! Up and out!'

'But . . . but . . . but . . . it's made of glass!' shouted Grandpa Joe. 'It'll break into a million pieces!'

'I suppose it might,' said Mr Wonka, cheerful as ever, 'but it's pretty thick glass, all the same.'

The lift rushed on, going up and up and up, faster and faster and faster . . .

Then suddenly, *CRASH!* – and the most tremendous noise of splintering wood and broken tiles came from directly above their heads, and Grandpa Joe shouted, 'Help! It's the end! We're done for!' and Mr Wonka said, 'No, we're not! We're through! We're out!' Sure enough, the lift had shot right up through the roof of the factory and was now rising into the sky like a rocket, and the sunshine was pouring in through the glass roof. In five seconds they were a thousand feet up in the sky.

'The lift's gone mad!' shouted Grandpa Joe.

176

'Have no fear, my dear sir,' said Mr Wonka calmly, and he pressed another button. The lift stopped. It stopped and hung in mid-air, hovering like a helicopter, hovering over the factory and over the very town itself which lay spread out below them like a picture postcard! Looking down through the glass floor on which he was standing, Charlie could see the small far-away houses and the streets and the snow that lay thickly over everything. It was an eerie and frightening feeling to be standing on clear glass high up in the sky. It made you feel that you weren't standing on anything at all.

'Are we all right?' cried Grandpa Joe. 'How does this thing stay up?'

'Sugar power!' said Mr Wonka. 'One million sugar power! Oh, look,' he cried, pointing down, 'there go the other children! They're returning home!'

29

The Other Children Go Home

'We *must* go down and take a look at our little friends before we do anything else,' said Mr Wonka. He pressed a different button, and the lift dropped lower, and soon it was hovering just above the entrance gates to the factory.

Looking down now, Charlie could see the children and their parents standing in a little group just inside the gates.

'I can only see three,' he said. 'Who's missing?'

'I expect it's Mike Teavee,' Mr Wonka said. 'But he'll be coming along soon. Do you see the trucks?' Mr Wonka pointed to a line of gigantic covered vans parked in a line near by.

'Yes,' Charlie said. 'What are *they* for?'

'Don't you remember what it said on the Golden Tickets? Every child goes home with a lifetime's supply of sweets. There's one truckload for each of them, loaded to the brim. Ah-ha,' Mr Wonka went on, 'there goes our friend Augustus Gloop! D'you see him? He's getting into the first truck with his mother and father!'

'You mean he's *really* all right?' asked Charlie, astonished. 'Even after going up that awful pipe?'

'He's very much all right,' said Mr Wonka.

'He's changed!' said Grandpa Joe, peering down through the glass wall of the elevator. 'He used to be fat! Now he's thin as a straw!'

'Of course he's changed,' said Mr Wonka, laughing. 'He got squeezed in the pipe. Don't you remember? And look! There goes Miss Violet Beauregarde, the great gum-chewer! It seems as though they managed to de-juice her after all. I'm so glad. And how healthy she looks! Much better than before!'

'But she's purple in the face!' cried Grandpa Joe.

'So she is,' said Mr Wonka. 'Ah, well, there's nothing we can do about that.'

'Good gracious!' cried Charlie. 'Look at poor

Veruca Salt and Mr Salt and Mrs Salt! They're simply *covered* with rubbish!'

'And here comes Mike Teavee!' said Grandpa Joe. 'Good heavens! What have they done to him? He's about ten feet tall and thin as a wire!'

'They've overstretched him on the gum-stretching machine,' said Mr Wonka. 'How very careless.'

'But how dreadful for him!' cried Charlie.

'Nonsense,' said Mr Wonka, 'he's very lucky. Every basketball team in the country will be trying to get him. But now,' he added, 'it is time we left these four silly children. I have something very important to talk to you about, my dear Charlie.' Mr Wonka pressed another button, and the lift swung upwards into the sky.

Charlie's Chocolate Factory

The great glass lift was now hovering high over the town. Inside the lift stood Mr Wonka, Grandpa Joe, and little Charlie.

'How I love my chocolate factory,' said Mr Wonka, gazing down. Then he paused, and he turned around and looked at Charlie with a most serious expression on his face. 'Do *you* love it too, Charlie?' he asked.

'Oh, yes,' cried Charlie, 'I think it's the most wonderful place in the whole world!'

'I am very pleased to hear you say that,' said Mr Wonka, looking more serious than ever. He went on staring at Charlie. 'Yes,' he said, 'I am very pleased indeed to hear you say that. And now I shall tell you why.' Mr Wonka cocked his head to one side and all at once the tiny twinkling wrinkles of a smile appeared around the corners of his eyes, and he said, 'You see, my dear boy, I have decided to make you a present of the whole place. As soon as you are old enough to run it, the entire factory will become yours.'

Charlie stared at Mr Wonka. Grandpa Joe

opened his mouth to speak, but no words came out.

'It's quite true,' Mr Wonka said, smiling broadly now. 'I really am giving it to you. That's all right, isn't it?'

'*Giving* it to him?' gasped Grandpa Joe. 'You must be joking.'

'I'm not joking, sir. I'm deadly serious.'

'But ... but ... why should you want to give your factory to little Charlie?'

'Listen,' Mr Wonka said, 'I'm an old man. I'm much older than you think. I can't go on for ever. I've got no children of my own, no family at all. So who is going to run the factory when I get too old to do it myself? *Someone's* got to keep it going – if only for the sake of the Oompa-Loompas. Mind you, there are thousands of clever men who would give anything for the chance to come in and take over from me, but I don't want that sort of person. I don't want a grown-up person at all. A grown-up won't listen to me; he won't learn. He will try to do things his own way and not mine. So I have to have a child. I want a good sensible loving child, one to whom I can tell all my most precious sweet-making secrets – while I am still alive.'

'*So that* is why you sent out the Golden Tickets!' cried Charlie.

'Exactly!' said Mr Wonka. 'I decided to invite five children to the factory, and the one I liked best at the end of the day would be the winner!'

'But Mr Wonka,' stammered Grandpa Joe, 'do you really and truly mean that you are giving the whole of this enormous factory to little Charlie? After all . . .'

'There's no time for arguments!' cried Mr Wonka. 'We must go at once and fetch the rest of the family – Charlie's father and his mother and anyone else that's around! They can all live in the factory from now on! They can all help to run it until Charlie is old enough to do it by himself! Where do you live, Charlie?'

Charlie peered down through the glass floor at the snow-covered houses that lay below. 'It's over there,' he said, pointing. 'It's that little cottage right on the edge of the town, the tiny little one . . .'

'I see it!' cried Mr Wonka, and he pressed some more buttons and the lift shot down towards Charlie's house.

'I'm afraid my mother won't come with us,' Charlie said sadly.

'Why ever not?'

'Because she won't leave Grandma Josephine and Grandma Georgina and Grandpa George.'

'But they must come too.'

'They can't,' Charlie said. 'They're very old and they haven't been out of bed for twenty years.'

'Then we'll take the bed along as well, with them in it,' said Mr Wonka. 'There's plenty of room in this lift for a bed.'

'You couldn't get the bed out of the house,' said Grandpa Joe. 'It won't go through the door.'

'You mustn't despair!' cried Mr Wonka. 'Nothing is impossible! You watch!'

The lift was now hovering over the roof of the Buckets' little house.

'What are you going to do?' cried Charlie.

'I'm going right on in to fetch them,' said Mr Wonka.

'How?' asked Grandpa Joe.

'Through the roof,' said Mr Wonka, pressing another button.

'No!' shouted Charlie.

'Stop!' shouted Grandpa Joe.

CRASH went the lift, right down through the roof of the house into the old people's bedroom. Showers of dust and broken tiles and bits of wood and cockroaches and spiders and bricks and cement went raining down on the three old ones who were lying in bed, and each of them thought that the end of the world was come. Grandma Georgina fainted, Grandma Josephine dropped her false teeth, Grandpa George put his head under the blanket, and Mr and Mrs Bucket came rushing in from the next room.

'Save us!' cried Grandma Josephine.

'Calm yourself, my darling wife,' said Grandpa Joe, stepping out of the lift. 'It's only us.'

'Mother!' cried Charlie, rushing into Mrs Bucket's arms. 'Mother! Mother! Listen to what's happened! We're all going back to live in Mr Wonka's factory and we're going to help him to run it and he's given it *all* to me and . . . and . . . and . . . and . . .'

'What *are* you talking about?' said Mrs Bucket.

'Just look at our house!' cried poor Mr Bucket. 'It's in ruins!'

'My dear sir,' said Mr Wonka, jumping forward and shaking Mr Bucket warmly by the hand, 'I'm so very glad to meet you. You mustn't worry about your house. From now on, you're never going to need it again, anyway.'

'Who *is* this crazy man?' screamed Grandma Josephine. 'He could have killed us all.'

'This,' said Grandpa Joe, 'is Mr Willy Wonka himself.'

It took quite a time for Grandpa Joe and Charlie to explain to everyone exactly what had been happening to them all day. And even then they all refused to ride back to the factory in the lift.

'I'd rather die in my bed!' shouted Grandma Josephine.

'So would I!' cried Grandma Georgina.

'I refuse to go!' announced Grandpa George.

So Mr Wonka and Grandpa Joe and Charlie, taking no notice of their screams, simply pushed the bed into the lift. They pushed Mr and Mrs Bucket in after it. Then they got in themselves. Mr Wonka pressed a button. The doors closed. Grandma Georgina screamed. And the lift rose up off the floor and shot through the hole in the roof, out into the open sky.

Charlie climbed on to the bed and tried to calm the three old people who were still petrified with fear. 'Please don't be frightened,' he said. 'It's quite safe. And we're going to the most wonderful place in the world!'

'Charlie's right,' said Grandpa Joe.

'Will there be anything to eat when we get

there?' asked Grandma Josephine. 'I'm starving! The whole family is starving!'

'Anything to *eat*?' cried Charlie laughing. 'Oh, you just wait and see!'

James and the Giant Peach

*This book
is for Olivia and Tessa*

One

Until he was four years old, James Henry Trotter had a happy life. He lived peacefully with his mother and father in a beautiful house beside the sea. There were always plenty of other children for him to play with, and there was the sandy beach for him to run about on, and the ocean to paddle in. It was the perfect life for a small boy.

Then, one day, James's mother and father went to London to do some shopping, and there a terrible thing happened. Both of them suddenly got eaten up (in full daylight, mind you, and on a crowded street) by an enormous angry rhinoceros which had escaped from the London Zoo.

Now this, as you can well imagine, was a rather nasty experience for two such gentle parents. But in the long run it was far nastier for James than it was for them. *Their* troubles were all over in a jiffy. They were dead and gone in thirty-five seconds flat. Poor James, on the other hand, was still very much alive, and all at once he found himself alone and frightened in a vast unfriendly world. The lovely house by the seaside had to be sold immediately, and the little boy, carrying nothing but a small suitcase containing a pair of pyjamas and a toothbrush, was sent away to live with his two aunts.

Their names were Aunt Sponge and Aunt Spiker, and I am sorry to say that they were both really horrible people. They were selfish and lazy and cruel, and right from the beginning they started beating poor James for almost no reason at all. They never called him by his real name, but always referred to him as 'you disgusting little beast' or 'you filthy nuisance' or 'you miserable creature', and they certainly never gave him any toys to play with or any picture books to look at. His room was as bare as a prison cell.

They livcd – Aunt Sponge, Aunt Spiker, and now James as well – in a queer ramshackle house on the top of a high hill in the south of England. The hill was so high that from almost anywhere in the garden James could look down and see for miles and miles across a marvellous landscape of

woods and fields; and on a very clear day, if he
looked in the right direction, he could see a tiny
grey dot far away on the horizon, which was the
house that he used to live in with his beloved
mother and father. And just beyond that, he could
see the ocean itself – a long thin streak of blackish-
blue, like a line of ink, beneath the rim of the sky.

But James was never allowed to go down off the
top of that hill. Neither Aunt Sponge nor Aunt
Spiker could ever be bothered to take him out
herself, not even for a small walk or a picnic, and
he certainly wasn't permitted to go alone. 'The
nasty little beast will only get into mischief if he
goes out of the garden,' Aunt Spiker had said. And

terrible punishments were promised him, such as being locked up in the cellar with the rats for a week, if he even so much as dared to climb over the fence.

The garden, which covered the whole of the top of the hill, was large and desolate, and the only tree in the entire place (apart from a clump of dirty old laurel bushes at the far end) was an ancient peach tree that never gave any peaches. There was no swing, no seesaw, no sand pit, and no other children were ever invited to come up the hill to play with poor James. There wasn't so much as a dog or a cat around to keep him company. And as time went on, he became sadder and sadder, and more and more lonely, and he used to spend hours every day standing at the bottom of the

garden, gazing wistfully at the lovely but forbidden world of woods and fields and ocean that was spread out below him like a magic carpet.

Two

After James Henry Trotter had been living with his aunts for three whole years there came a morning when something rather peculiar happened to him. And this thing, which as I say was only *rather* peculiar, soon caused a second thing to happen which was *very* peculiar. And then the *very* peculiar thing, in its own turn, caused a really *fantastically* peculiar thing to occur.

It all started on a blazing hot day in the middle of summer. Aunt Sponge, Aunt Spiker and James were all out in the garden. James had been put to work, as usual. This time he was chopping wood for the kitchen stove. Aunt Sponge and Aunt Spiker were sitting comfortably in deck-chairs near by, sipping tall glasses of fizzy lemonade and watching him to see that he didn't stop work for one moment.

Aunt Sponge was enormously fat and very short. She had small piggy eyes, a sunken mouth, and one of those white flabby faces that looked exactly as though it had been boiled. She was like a great white soggy overboiled cabbage. Aunt Spiker, on the other hand, was lean and tall and bony, and she wore steel-rimmed spectacles that fixed on to the end of her nose with a clip. She had a screeching voice and long wet narrow lips, and whenever she got angry or excited, little flecks of spit would come shooting out of her mouth as she talked. And there they sat, these two ghastly hags, sipping their drinks, and every now and again screaming at James to chop faster and faster. They also talked about themselves, each one saying how beautiful she thought she was. Aunt

Sponge had a long-handled mirror on her lap, and she kept picking it up and gazing at her own hideous face.

'I look and smell,' Aunt Sponge declared, 'as lovely as
a rose!
Just feast your eyes upon my face, observe my shapely
nose!
Behold my heavenly silky locks!
And if I take off both my socks
You'll see my dainty toes.'
'But don't forget,' Aunt Spiker cried, 'how much your
tummy shows!'

Aunt Sponge went red. Aunt Spiker said, 'My sweet,
you cannot win,
Behold MY gorgeous curvy shape, my teeth, my charm-
ing grin!
Oh, beauteous me! How I adore
My radiant looks! And please ignore
The pimple on my chin.'
'My dear old trout!' Aunt Sponge cried out, 'You're
only bones and skin!'

'Such loveliness as I possess can only truly shine
In Hollywood!' Aunt Sponge declared: 'Oh, wouldn't
that be fine!
I'd capture all the nations' hearts!
They'd give me all the leading parts!
The stars would all resign!'
'I think you'd make,' Aunt Spiker said, 'a lovely
Frankenstein.'

Poor James was still slaving away at the chopping-block. The heat was terrible. He was sweating all over. His arm was aching. The chopper was a large blunt thing far too heavy for a small boy to use. And as he worked, James began thinking about all the other children in the world and what they might be doing at this moment. Some would be riding tricycles in their gardens. Some would be walking in cool woods and picking bunches of wild flowers. And all the little friends whom he used to know would be down by the seaside, playing in the wet sand and splashing around in the water . . .

Great tears began oozing out of James's eyes and

rolling down his cheeks. He stopped working and leaned against the chopping-block, overwhelmed by his own unhappiness.

'What's the matter with you?' Aunt Spiker screeched, glaring at him over the top of her steel spectacles.

James began to cry.

'Stop that immediately and get on with your work, you nasty little beast!' Aunt Sponge ordered.

'Oh, Auntie Sponge!' James cried out. 'And Auntie Spiker! Couldn't we all – *please* – just for once – go down to the seaside on the bus? It isn't very far – and I feel so hot and awful and lonely . . .'

'Why, you lazy good-for-nothing brute!' Aunt Spiker shouted.

'Beat him!' cried Aunt Sponge.

'I certainly will!' Aunt Spiker snapped. She glared at James, and James looked back at her with large frightened eyes. 'I shall beat you later on in the day when I don't feel so hot,' she said. 'And now get out of my sight, you disgusting little worm, and give me some peace!'

James turned and ran. He ran off as fast as he could to the far end of the garden and hid himself behind that clump of dirty old laurel bushes that we mentioned earlier on. Then he covered his face with his hands and began to cry and cry.

Three

It was at this point that the first thing of all, the *rather* peculiar thing that led to so many other *much* more peculiar things, happened to him.

For suddenly, just behind him, James heard a rustling of leaves, and he turned round and saw an old man in a funny dark-green suit emerging from the bushes. He was a very small old man, but he had a huge bald head and a face that was covered all over with bristly black whiskers. He stopped when he was about three yards away, and he stood there leaning on his stick and staring hard at James.

When he spoke, his voice was very slow and creaky. 'Come closer to me, little boy,' he said, beckoning to James with a finger. 'Come right up close to me and I will show you something *wonderful*.'

James was too frightened to move.

The old man hobbled a step or two nearer, and then he put a hand into the pocket of his jacket and took out a small white paper bag.

'You see this?' he whispered, waving the bag gently to and fro in front of James's face. 'You know what this is, my dear? You know what's inside this little bag?'

Then he came nearer still, leaning forward and pushing his face so close to James that James could feel breath blowing on his cheeks. The breath

smelled musty and stale and slightly mildewed, like air in an old cellar.

'Take a look, my dear,' he said, opening the bag and tilting it towards James. Inside it, James could see a mass of tiny green things that looked like little stones or crystals, each one about the size of a grain of rice. They were extraordinarily beautiful, and there was a strange brightness about them, a sort of luminous quality that made them glow and sparkle in the most wonderful way.

'Listen to them!' the old man whispered. 'Listen to them move!'

James stared into the bag, and sure enough there was a faint rustling sound coming up from inside it, and then he noticed that all the thousands of little green things were slowly, very very slowly stirring about and moving over each other as though they were alive.

'There's more power and magic in those things in there than in all the rest of the world put together,' the old man said softly.

'But – but – what *are* they?' James murmured, finding his voice at last. 'Where do they come from?'

'Ah-ha,' the old man whispered. 'You'd never guess that!' He was crouching a little now and pushing his face still closer and closer to James until the tip of his long nose was actually touching the skin on James's forehead. Then suddenly he jumped back and began waving his stick madly in the air. 'Crocodile tongues!' he cried. 'One thousand long slimy crocodile tongues boiled up in the skull of a dead witch for twenty days and nights with the eyeballs of a lizard! Add the fingers of a young monkey, the gizzard of a pig, the beak of a green parrot, the juice of a porcupine, and three spoonfuls of sugar. Stew for another week, and then let the moon do the rest!'

All at once, he pushed the white paper bag into James's hands, and said, 'Here! You take it! It's yours!'

Four

James Henry Trotter stood there clutching the bag and staring at the old man.

'And now,' the old man said, 'all you've got to do is this. Take a large jug of water, and pour all the little green things into it. Then, very slowly, one by one, add ten hairs from your own head. That sets them off! It gets them going! In a couple of minutes the water will begin to froth and bubble furiously, and as soon as that happens you must quickly drink it all down, the whole jugful, in one gulp. And then, my dear, you will feel it churning and boiling in your stomach, and steam will start coming out of your mouth, and immediately after that, *marvellous* things will start happening to you, *fabulous*, *unbelievable* things – and you will never be miserable again in your life. Because you *are* miserable, aren't you? You needn't tell me! I know *all* about it! Now, off you go and do exactly as I say. And don't whisper a word of this to those two horrible aunts of yours! Not a word! And don't let those green things in there get away from you either! Because if they do escape, then they will be working their magic upon somebody else instead of upon *you*! And that isn't what you want at all, is it, my dear? *Whoever they meet first, be it bug, insect, animal, or tree, that will be the one who gets the full power of their magic!* So hold the bag tight! Don't tear the paper! Off you go! Hurry up! Don't wait! Now's the time! Hurry!'

With that, the old man turned away and disappeared into the bushes.

Five

The next moment, James was running back towards the house as fast as he could go. He would do it all in the kitchen, he told himself – if only he could get in there without Aunt Sponge and Aunt Spiker seeing him. He was terribly excited. He flew through the long grass and the stinging-nettles, not caring whether he got stung or not on his bare knees, and in the distance he could see Aunt Sponge and Aunt Spiker sitting in their chairs with their backs towards him. He swerved away from them so as to go round the other side of the house, but then suddenly, just as he was passing underneath the old peach tree that stood in the middle of the garden, his foot slipped and he fell flat on his face in the grass. The paper bag burst open as it hit the ground and the thousands of tiny green things were scattered in all directions.

James immediately picked himself up on to his

hands and knees and started searching around for his precious treasures. *But what was this?* They were all sinking into the soil! He could actually see them wriggling and twisting as they burrowed their way downward into the hard earth, and at once he reached out a hand to pick some of them up before it was too late, but they disappeared right under his fingers. He went after some others, and the same thing happened! He began scrabbling around frantically in an effort to catch hold of those that were left, but they were too quick for him. Each time the tips of his fingers were just about to touch them, they vanished into the earth! And soon, in the space of only a few seconds, every single one of them had gone!

James felt like crying. He would never get them back now – they were lost, lost, lost for ever.

But where had they gone to? And why in the world had they been so eager to push down into the earth like that? What were they after? There was nothing down *there*. Nothing except the roots of the old peach tree . . . and a whole lot of earthworms and centipedes and insects living in the soil.

But what was it that the old man had said? *Whoever they meet first, be it bug, insect, animal, or tree, that will be the one who gets the full power of their magic!*

Good heavens, thought James. What is going to happen in that case if they do meet an earthworm? Or a centipede? Or a spider? And what if they do go into the roots of the peach tree?

'Get up at once, you lazy little beast!' a voice was suddenly shouting in James's ear. James glanced up and saw Aunt Spiker standing over him, grim and tall and bony, glaring at him through her steel-rimmed spectacles. 'Get back over there immediately and finish chopping up those logs!' she ordered.

Aunt Sponge, fat and pulpy as a jellyfish, came waddling up behind her sister to see what was going on. 'Why don't we just lower the boy down the well in a bucket and leave him there for the night?' she suggested. 'That ought to teach him not to laze around like this the whole day long.'

'That's a very good wheeze, my dear Sponge. But let's make him finish chopping up the wood first. Be off with you at once, you hideous brat, and do some work!'

Slowly, sadly, poor James got up off the ground and went back to the woodpile. Oh, if only he hadn't slipped and fallen and dropped that precious bag. All hope of a happier life had gone completely now. Today and tomorrow and the next day and all the other days as well would be nothing but punishment and pain, unhappiness and despair.

He picked up the chopper and was just about to start chopping away again when he heard a shout behind him that made him stop and turn.

Six

'Sponge! Sponge! Come here at once and look at this!'

'At what?'

'It's a peach!' Aunt Spiker was shouting.

'A what?'

'A peach! Right up there on the highest branch!
Can't you see it?'

'I think you must be mistaken, my dear Spiker.
That miserable tree *never* has any peaches on it.'

'There's one on it now, Sponge! You look for
yourself!'

'You're teasing me, Spiker. You're making my

mouth water on purpose when there's nothing to put into it. Why, that tree's never even had a *blossom* on it, let alone a peach. Right up on the highest branch, you say? I can't see a thing. Very funny ... Ha, ha ... *Good gracious* me! Well, *I'll be blowed!* There really *is* a peach up there!'

'A nice big one, too!' Aunt Spiker said.

'A beauty, a beauty!' Aunt Sponge cried out.

At this point, James slowly put down his chopper and turned and looked across at the two women who were standing underneath the peach tree.

Something is about to happen, he told himself. *Something peculiar is about to happen any moment*. He hadn't the faintest idea what it might be, but he could feel it in his bones that something was going to happen soon. He could feel it in the air around him ... in the sudden stillness that had fallen upon the garden ...

James tiptoed a little closer to the tree. The aunts were not talking now. They were just standing there, staring at the peach. There was not a sound anywhere, not even a breath of wind, and overhead the sun blazed down upon them out of a deep blue sky.

'It looks ripe to me,' Aunt Spiker said, breaking the silence.

'Then why don't we eat it?' Aunt Sponge suggested, licking her thick lips. 'We can have half each. Hey, you! James! Come over here at once and climb this tree!'

James came running over.

'I want you to pick that peach up there on the

highest branch,' Aunt Sponge went on. 'Can you see it?'

'Yes, Auntie Sponge, I can see it!'

'And don't you dare eat any of it yourself. Your Aunt Spiker and I are going to have it between us right here and now, half each. Get on with you! Up you go!'

James crossed over to the tree trunk.

'Stop!' Aunt Spiker said quickly. 'Hold everything!' She was staring up into the branches with her mouth wide open and her eyes bulging as though she had seen a ghost. '*Look!*' she said. '*Look*, Sponge, *look!*'

'What's the matter with you?' Aunt Sponge demanded.

'It's *growing*!' Aunt Spiker cried. 'It's getting bigger and bigger!'

'What is?'

'The peach, of course!'

'You're joking!'

'Well, look for yourself!'

'But my dear Spiker, that's perfectly ridiculous. That's impossible. That's – that's – that's – Now, wait *just* a minute – No – No – that can't be right – No – Yes – Great Scott! The thing really *is* growing!'

'It's nearly twice as big already!' Aunt Spiker shouted.

'It can't be true!'

'It is true!'

'It must be a miracle!'

'Watch it! Watch it!'

'I am watching it!'

'Great heavens alive!' Aunt Spiker yelled. 'I can actually see the thing bulging and swelling before my very eyes!'

Seven

The two women and the small boy stood absolutely still on the grass underneath the tree, gazing up at this extraordinary fruit. James's little face was glowing with excitement, his eyes were as big and bright as two stars. He could see the peach swelling larger and larger as clearly as if it were a balloon being blown up.

In half a minute, it was the size of a melon!

In another half-minute, it was *twice* as big again!

'Just *look* at it growing!' Aunt Spiker cried.

'Will it ever stop!' Aunt Sponge shouted, waving her fat arms and starting to dance around in circles.

And now it was so big it looked like an enormous butter-coloured pumpkin dangling from the top of the tree.

'Get away from that tree trunk, you stupid boy!' Aunt Spiker yelled. 'The slightest shake and I'm sure it'll fall off! It must weigh twenty or thirty pounds at least!'

The branch that the peach was growing upon was beginning to bend over further and further.

because of the weight.

'Stand back!' Aunt Sponge shouted. 'It's coming down! The branch is going to break!'

But the branch didn't break. It simply bent over more and more as the peach got heavier and heavier.

And still it went on growing.

In another minute, this mammoth fruit was as large and round and fat as Aunt Sponge herself, and probably just as heavy.

'It *has* to stop now!' Aunt Spiker yelled. 'It can't go on for ever!'

But it didn't stop.

Soon it was the size of a small car, and reached halfway to the ground.

Both aunts were now hopping round and round the tree, clapping their hands and shouting all sorts of silly things in their excitement.

'Hallelujah!' Aunt Spiker shouted. 'What a peach! What a peach!'

'Terrifico!' Aunt Sponge cried out, 'Magnifico! Splendifico! And what a meal!'

'It's still growing.'

'I know! I know!'

As for James, he was so spellbound by the whole thing that he could only stand and stare and murmur quietly to himself, 'Oh, isn't it beautiful. It's the most beautiful thing I've ever seen.'

'Shut up, you little twerp!' Aunt Spiker snapped, happening to overhear him. 'It's none of your business!'

'That's right,' Aunt Sponge declared. 'It's got nothing to do with you whatsoever! Keep out of it.'

'Look!' Aunt Spiker shouted. 'It's growing faster than ever now! It's speeding up!'

'I see it, Spiker! I do! I do!'

Bigger and bigger grew the peach, bigger and bigger and bigger.

Then at last, when it had become nearly as tall as the tree that it was growing on, as tall and wide, in fact, as a small house, the bottom part of it gently touched the ground – and there it rested.

'It can't fall off now!' Aunt Sponge shouted.

'It's stopped growing!' Aunt Spiker cried.

'No, it hasn't!'

'Yes, it has!'

'It's slowing down, Spiker, it's slowing down! But it hasn't stopped yet! You watch it!'

There was a pause.

'It has now!'

'I believe you're right.'

'Do you think it's safe to touch it?'

'I don't know. We'd better be careful.'

Aunt Sponge and Aunt Spiker began walking slowly round the peach, inspecting it very cautiously from all sides. They were like a couple of hunters who had just shot an elephant and were not quite sure whether it was dead or alive. And the massive round fruit towered over them so high that they looked like midgets from another world beside it.

The skin of the peach was very beautiful – a rich buttery yellow with patches of brilliant pink and red. Aunt Sponge advanced cautiously and touched it with the tip of one finger. 'It's ripe!' she cried. 'It's just perfect! Now, look here, Spiker. Why don't we go and get a shovel right away and dig out a great big chunk of it for you and me to eat?'

'No,' Aunt Spiker said. 'Not yet.'

'Why ever not?'

'Because I say so.'

'But I can't *wait* to eat some!' Aunt Sponge cried out. She was watering at the mouth now and a thin trickle of spit was running down one side of her chin.

'My dear Sponge,' Aunt Spiker said slowly, winking at her sister and smiling a sly, thin-lipped smile. 'There's a pile of money to be made out of this if only we can handle it right. You wait and see.'

Eight

The news that a peach almost as big as a house had suddenly appeared in someone's garden spread like wildfire across the countryside, and the next day a stream of people came scrambling up the steep hill to gaze upon this marvel.

Quickly, Aunt Sponge and Aunt Spiker called in carpenters and had them build a strong fence round the peach to save it from the crowd; and at the same time, these two crafty women stationed themselves at the front gate with a large bunch of tickets

219

and started charging everyone for coming in.

'Roll up! Roll up!' Aunt Spiker yelled. 'Only one shilling to see the giant peach!'

'Half price for children under six weeks old!' Aunt Sponge shouted.

'One at a time, please! Don't push! Don't push! You're all going to get in!'

'Hey, you! Come back, there! You haven't paid!'

By lunchtime, the whole place was a seething mass of men, women, and children all pushing and shoving to get a glimpse of this miraculous fruit. Helicopters were landing like wasps all over the hill, and out of them poured swarms of newspaper reporters, cameramen, and men from the television companies.

'It'll cost you double to bring in a camera!' Aunt Spiker shouted.

'All right! All right!' they answered. 'We don't care!' And the money came rolling into the pockets of the two greedy aunts.

But while all this excitement was going on out-side, poor James was forced to stay locked in his bedroom, peeping through the bars of his window at the crowds below.

'The disgusting little brute will only get in every-one's way if we let him wander about,' Aunt Spiker had said early that morning.

'Oh, *please!*' he had begged. 'I haven't met any other children for years and years and there are going to be lots of them down there for me to play with. And perhaps I could help you with the tickets.'

'Shut up!' Aunt Sponge had snapped. 'Your Aunt Spiker and I are about to become millionaires, and the last thing we want is the likes of you messing things up and getting in the way.'

Later, when the evening of the first day came and the people had all gone home, the aunts unlocked James's door and ordered him to go outside and pick up all the banana skins and orange peel and bits of paper that the crowd had left behind.

'Could I please have something to eat first?' he asked. 'I haven't had a thing all day.'

'No!' they shouted, kicking him out of the door. 'We're too busy to make food! We are counting our money!'

'But it's dark!' cried James.

'Get out!' they yelled. 'And stay out until you've cleaned up all the mess!' The door slammed. The key turned in the lock.

Nine

Hungry and trembling, James stood alone out in the open, wondering what to do. The night was all around him now, and high overhead a wild white moon was riding in the sky. There was not a sound, not a movement anywhere.

Most people – and especially small children – are often quite scared of being out of doors alone in the moonlight. Everything is so deadly quiet, and

the shadows are so long and black, and they keep turning into strange shapes that seem to move as you look at them, and the slightest little snap of a twig makes you jump.

James felt exactly like that now. He stared straight ahead with large frightened eyes, hardly daring to breathe. Not far away, in the middle of the garden, he could see the giant peach towering over everything else. Surely it was even bigger tonight than ever before? And what a dazzling sight it was! The moonlight was shining and glinting on its great curving sides, turning them to crystal and silver. It looked like a tremendous silver ball lying there in the grass, silent, mysterious, and wonderful.

And then all at once, little shivers of excitement started running over the skin on James's back.

Something else, he told himself, *something stranger than ever this time, is about to happen to me again soon.* He was sure of it. He could feel it coming.

He looked around him, wondering what on earth it was going to be. The garden lay soft and silver in the moonlight. The grass was wet with dew and a million dewdrops were sparkling and twinkling like diamonds around his feet. And now suddenly, the whole place, the whole garden seemed to be *alive* with magic.

Almost without knowing what he was doing, as though drawn by some powerful magnet, James Henry Trotter started walking slowly towards the giant peach. He climbed over the fence that surrounded it, and stood directly beneath it, staring up at its great bulging sides. He put out a hand and touched it gently with the tip of one finger. It felt soft and warm and slightly furry, like the skin of a baby mouse. He moved a step closer and rubbed his cheek lightly against the soft skin. And then suddenly, while he was doing this, he happened to notice that right beside him and below him, close to the ground, there was a hole in the side of the peach.

Ten

It was quite a large hole, the sort of thing an animal about the size of a fox might have made.

James knelt down in front of it, and poked his head and shoulders inside.

He crawled in.

He kept on crawling.

This isn't a hole, he thought excitedly. *It's a tunnel!*

The tunnel was damp and murky, and all around him there was the curious bittersweet smell of fresh peach. The floor was soggy under his knees, the walls were wet and sticky, and peach juice was dripping from the ceiling. James opened his mouth and caught some of it on his tongue. It tasted delicious.

He was crawling uphill now, as though the tunnel were leading straight towards the very centre of the gigantic fruit. Every few seconds he

225

paused and took a bite out of the wall. The peach flesh was sweet and juicy, and marvellously refreshing.

He crawled on for several more yards, and then suddenly – *bang* – the top of his head bumped into something extremely hard blocking his way. He glanced up. In front of him there was a solid wall that seemed at first as though it were made of wood. He touched it with his fingers. It certainly felt like wood, except that it was very jagged and full of deep grooves.

'Good heavens!' he said. 'I know what this is! I've come to the stone in the middle of the peach!'

Then he noticed that there was a small door cut into the face of the peach stone. He gave a push. It swung open. He crawled through it, and before he had time to glance up and see where he was, he

heard a voice saying, '*Look* who's here!' And another one said, 'We've been *waiting* for you!'

James stopped and stared at the speakers, his face white with horror.

He started to stand up, but his knees were shaking so much he had to sit down again on the floor. He glanced behind him, thinking he could bolt back into the tunnel the way he had come, but the doorway had disappeared. There was now only a solid brown wall behind him.

Eleven

James's large frightened eyes travelled slowly round the room.

The creatures, some sitting on chairs, others reclining on a sofa, were all watching him intently.

Creatures?

Or were they insects?

An insect is usually something rather small, is it not? A grasshopper, for example, is an insect.

So what would you call it if you saw a grasshopper as large as a dog? As large as a *large* dog. You could hardly call *that* an insect, could you?

There was an Old-Green-Grasshopper as large as a large dog sitting directly across the room from James now.

And next to the Old-Green-Grasshopper, there was an enormous Spider.

And next to the Spider, there was a giant Ladybird with nine black spots on her scarlet shell.

Each of these three was squatting upon a magnificent chair.

On a sofa near by, reclining comfortably in
curled-up positions, there were a Centipede and an
Earthworm.

On the floor over in the far corner, there was
something thick and white that looked as though it
might be a Silkworm. But it was sleeping soundly
and nobody was paying any attention to it.

Every one of these 'creatures' was at least as big as James himself, and in the strange greenish light that shone down from somewhere in the ceiling, they were absolutely terrifying to behold.

'I'm hungry!' the Spider announced suddenly, staring hard at James.

'*I'm* famished!' the Old-Green-Grasshopper said.

'So am *I*!' the Ladybird cried.

The Centipede sat up a little straighter on the sofa. '*Everyone's* famished!' he said. 'We need food!'

Four pairs of round black glassy eyes were all fixed upon James.

The Centipede made a wriggling movement with his body as though he were about to glide off the sofa – but he didn't.

There was a long pause – and a long silence.

The Spider (who happened to be a female spider) opened her mouth and ran a long black tongue delicately over her lips. 'Aren't *you* hungry?' she asked suddenly, leaning forward and addressing herself to James.

Poor James was backed up against the far wall, shivering with fright and much too terrified to answer.

'What's the matter with you?' the Old-Green-Grasshopper asked. 'You look positively ill!'

'He looks as though he's going to faint any second,' the Centipede said.

'Oh, my goodness, the poor thing!' the Ladybird cried. 'I do believe he thinks it's *him* that we are wanting to eat!'

There was a roar of laughter from all sides.

'Oh dear, oh dear!' they said. 'What an awful thought!'

'You mustn't be frightened,' the Ladybird said kindly. 'We wouldn't *dream* of hurting you. You are one of *us* now, didn't you know that? You are one of the crew. We're all in the same boat.'

'We've been waiting for you all day long,' the Old-Green-Grasshopper said. 'We thought you were never going to turn up. I'm glad you made it.'

230

'So cheer up, my boy, cheer up!' the Centipede said. 'And meanwhile I wish you'd come over here and give me a hand with these boots. It takes me *hours* to get them all off by myself.'

Twelve

James decided that this was most certainly not a time to be disagreeable, so he crossed the room to where the Centipede was sitting and knelt down beside him.

'Thank you so much,' the Centipede said. 'You are very kind.'

'You have a lot of boots,' James murmured.

'I have a lot of legs,' the Centipede answered proudly. 'And a lot of feet. One hundred, to be exact.'

'*There* he goes again!' the Earthworm cried, speaking for the first time. 'He simply cannot stop telling lies about his legs! He doesn't have anything *like* a hundred of them! He's only got forty-two! The trouble is that most people don't bother to count them. They just take his word. And anyway, there is nothing *marvellous*, you know, Centipede, about having a lot of legs.'

'Poor fellow,' the Centipede said, whispering in James's ear. 'He's blind. He can't see how splendid I look.'

'In my opinion,' the Earthworm said, 'the *really*

marvellous thing is to have no legs at all and to be able to walk just the same.'

'You call that *walking!*' cried the Centipede. 'You're a *slitherer*, that's all you are! You just *slither* along!'

'I glide,' said the Earthworm primly.

'You are a slimy beast,' answered the Centipede.

'I am *not* a slimy beast,' the Earthworm said. 'I am a useful and much loved creature. Ask any gardener you like. And as for you . . .'

'I am a pest!' the Centipede announced, grinning broadly and looking round the room for approval.

'He is *so* proud of that,' the Ladybird said, smiling at James. 'Though for the life of me I cannot understand why.'

'I am the only pest in this room!' cried the Centipede, still grinning away. 'Unless you count Old-Green-Grasshopper over there. But he is long past it now. He is too old to be a pest any more.'

The Old-Green-Grasshopper turned his huge black eyes upon the Centipede and gave him a withering look. 'Young fellow,' he said, speaking in a deep, slow, scornful voice, 'I have never been a pest in my life. I am a musician.'

'Hear, hear!' said the Ladybird.

'James,' the Centipede said. 'Your name *is* James, isn't it?'

'Yes.'

'Well, James, have you ever in your life seen such a marvellous colossal Centipede as me?'

'I certainly haven't,' James answered. 'How on earth did you get to be like that?'

'*Very* peculiar,' the Centipede said. '*Very, very* peculiar indeed. Let me tell you what happened. I was messing about in the garden under the old peach tree and suddenly a funny little green thing came wriggling past my nose. Bright green it was, and extraordinarily beautiful, and it looked like some kind of a tiny stone or crystal . . .'

'Oh, but I know what that was!' cried James.

'It happened to me, too!' said the Ladybird.

'And me!' Miss Spider said. 'Suddenly there were little green things everywhere! The soil was full of them!'

'I actually swallowed one!' the Earthworm declared proudly.

'So did I!' the Ladybird said.

'I swallowed three!' the Centipede cried. 'But who's telling this story anyway? Don't interrupt!'

'It's too late to tell stories now,' the Old-Green-Grasshopper announced. 'It's time to go to sleep.'

'I refuse to sleep in my boots!' the Centipede cried. 'How many more are there to come off, James?'

'I think I've done about twenty so far,' James told him.

'Then that leaves eighty to go,' the Centipede said.

'*Twenty-two*, not *eighty!*' shrieked the Earthworm. 'He's lying again.'

The Centipede roared with laughter.

'Stop pulling the Earthworm's leg,' the Ladybird said.

This sent the Centipede into hysterics. 'Pulling his *leg!*' he cried, wriggling with glee and pointing at the Earthworm. 'Which leg am I pulling? You tell me that!'

James decided that he rather liked the Centipede. He was obviously a rascal, but what a change it was to hear somebody laughing once in a while. He had never heard Aunt Sponge or Aunt Spiker

laughing aloud in all the time he had been with
them.

'We really *must* get some sleep,' the Old-Green-
Grasshopper said. 'We've got a tough day ahead of
us tomorrow. So would you be kind enough, Miss
Spider, to make the beds?'

Thirteen

A few minutes later, Miss Spider had made the first
bed. It was hanging from the ceiling, suspended by
a rope of threads at either end so that actually it
looked more like a hammock than a bed. But it
was a magnificent affair, and the stuff that it was
made of shimmered like silk in the pale light.

'I do hope you'll find it comfortable,' Miss Spider
said to the Old-Green-Grasshopper. 'I made it as
soft and silky as I possibly could. I spun it with
gossamer. That's a much better quality thread
than the one I use for my own web.'

'Thank you so much, my dear lady,' the Old-
Green-Grasshopper said, climbing into the hammock. 'Ah, this is just what I needed. Good night,
everybody. Good night.'

Then Miss Spider spun the next hammock, and
the Ladybird got in.

After that, she spun a long one for the Centipede,
and an even longer one for the Earthworm.

'And how do you like *your* bed?' she said to

James when it came to his turn. 'Hard or soft?'

'I like it soft, thank you very much,' James answered.

'For goodness' sake stop staring round the room and get on with my boots!' the Centipede said. 'You and I are never going to get any sleep at this rate! And kindly line them up neatly in pairs as you take them off. Don't just throw them over your shoulder.'

James worked away frantically on the Centipede's boots. Each one had laces that had to be untied and loosened before it could be pulled off, and to make matters worse, all the laces were tied up in the most terrible complicated knots that had to be unpicked with fingernails. It was just awful. It took about two hours. And by the time James had pulled off the last boot of all and had lined them up in a row on the floor – twenty-one pairs altogether – the Centipede was fast asleep.

'Wake up, Centipede,' whispered James, giving him a gentle dig in the stomach. 'It's time for bed.'

'Thank you, my dear child,' the Centipede said, opening his eyes. Then he got down off the sofa and ambled across the room and crawled into his hammock. James got into his own hammock – and oh, how soft and comfortable it was compared with the hard bare boards that his aunts had always made him sleep upon at home.

'Lights out,' said the Centipede drowsily.

Nothing happened.

'Turn out the light!' he called, raising his voice.

James glanced round the room, wondering which

236

of the others he might be talking to, but they were all asleep. The Old-Green-Grasshopper was snoring loudly through his nose. The Ladybird was making whistling noises as she breathed, and the Earth-worm was coiled up like a spring at one end of his hammock, wheezing and blowing through his open mouth. As for Miss Spider, she had made a lovely web for herself across one corner of the room, and James could see her crouching right in the very centre of it, mumbling softly in her dreams.

'I said turn out the light!' shouted the Centipede angrily.

'Are you talking to me?' James asked him.

'Of course I'm not talking to you, you ass!' the Centipede answered. 'That crazy Glow-worm has gone to sleep with her light on!'

For the first time since entering the room, James glanced up at the ceiling – and there he saw a most extraordinary sight. Something that looked like a gigantic fly without wings (it was at least three feet long) was standing upside down upon its six legs in the middle of the ceiling, and the tail end of this creature seemed to be literally on fire. A brilliant greenish light as bright as the brightest electric bulb was shining out of its tail and lighting up the whole room.

'Is *that* a Glow-worm?' asked James, staring at the light. 'It doesn't look like a worm of any sort to me.'

'Of course it's a Glow-worm,' the Centipede answered. 'At least that's what *she* calls herself. Although actually you are quite right. She isn't

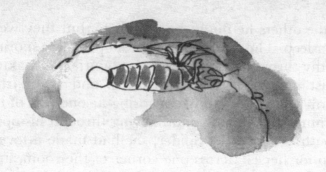

really a worm at all. Glow-worms are never worms. They are simply lady fireflies without wings. Wake up, you lazy beast!'

But the Glow-worm didn't stir, so the Centipede reached out of his hammock and picked up one of his boots from the floor. 'Put out that wretched light!' he shouted, hurling the boot up at the ceiling.

The Glow-worm slowly opened one eye and stared at the Centipede. 'There is no need to be rude,' she said coldly. 'All in good time.'

'Come on, come on, come on!' shouted the Centipede. 'Or I'll put it out for you!'

'Oh, hello, James!' the Glow-worm said, looking down and giving James a little wave and a smile. 'I didn't see you come in. Welcome, my dear boy, welcome – and good night!'

Then *click* – and out went the light.

James Henry Trotter lay there in the darkness with his eyes wide open, listening to the strange sleeping noises that the 'creatures' were making all around him, and wondering what on earth was going to happen to him in the morning. Already, he was beginning to like his new friends very much. They were not nearly as terrible as they looked. In fact they weren't really terrible at all. They seemed extremely kind and helpful in spite of all the shouting and arguing that went on between them.

'Good night, Old-Green-Grasshopper,' he whispered. 'Good night, Ladybird – Good night, Miss Spider – ' But before he could go through them all, he had fallen fast asleep.

Fourteen

'We're off!' someone was shouting. 'We're off at last!'

James woke up with a jump and looked about him. The creatures were all out of their hammocks and moving excitedly around the room. Suddenly,

239

the floor gave a great heave, as though an earth-quake were taking place.

'Here we go!' shouted the Old-Green-Grass-hopper, hopping up and down with excitement. 'Hold on tight!'

'What's happening?' cried James, leaping out of his hammock. 'What's going on?'

The Ladybird, who was obviously a kind and gentle creature, came over and stood beside him. 'In case you don't know it,' she said, 'we are about to depart for ever from the top of this ghastly hill that we've all been living on for so long. We are about to roll away inside this great big beautiful peach to a land of ... of ... of ... to a land of – '

'Of what?' asked James.

'Never you mind,' said the Ladybird. 'But nothing could be worse than this desolate hilltop and those two repulsive aunts of yours – '

'Hear, hear!' they all shouted. 'Hear, hear!'

'You may not have noticed it,' the Ladybird went on, 'but the whole garden, even before it reaches the steep edge of the hill, happens to be on a steep slope. And therefore the only thing that has been stopping this peach from rolling away right from the beginning is the thick stem attaching it to the tree. Break the stem, and off we go.'

'Watch it!' cried Miss Spider, as the room gave another violent lurch. 'Here we go!'

'Not quite! Not quite!'

'At this moment,' continued the Ladybird, 'our Centipede, who has a pair of jaws as sharp as razors, is up there on top of the peach nibbling

away at that stem. In fact, he must be nearly through it, as you can tell from the way we're lurching about. Would you like me to take you under my wing so that you won't fall over when we start rolling?'

'That's very kind of you,' said James, 'but I think I'll be all right.'

Just then, the Centipede stuck his grinning face through a hole in the ceiling and shouted, 'I've done it! We're off!'

'We're off!' the others cried. 'We're off!'

'The journey begins!' shouted the Centipede.

'And who knows where it will end,' muttered the Earthworm, 'if *you* have anything to do with it. It can only mean trouble.'

'Nonsense,' said the Ladybird. 'We are now about to visit the most marvellous places and see the most wonderful things! Isn't that so, Centipede?'

'There is no knowing what we shall see!' cried the Centipede.

'We may see a Creature with forty-nine heads
Who lives in the desolate snow,
And whenever he catches a cold (which he dreads)
He has forty-nine noses to blow.

'We may see the venomous Pink-Spotted Scrunch
Who can chew up a man with one bite.
It likes to eat five of them roasted for lunch
And eighteen for its supper at night.

'We may see a Dragon, and nobody knows
That we won't see a Unicorn there.
We may see a terrible Monster with toes
Growing out of the tufts of his hair.

'We may see the sweet little Biddy-Bright Hen
So playful, so kind and well-bred;
And such beautiful eggs! You just boil them and then
They explode and they blow off your head.

'A Gnu and a Gnocerous surely you'll see
And that gnormous and gnorrible Gnat
Whose sting when it stings you goes in at the knee
And comes out through the top of your hat.

'We may even get lost and be frozen by frost.
We may die in an earthquake or tremor.
Or nastier still, we may even be tossed
On the horns of a furious Dilemma.

'But who cares! Let us go from this horrible hill!
Let us roll! Let us bowl! Let us plunge!
Let's go rolling and bowling and spinning until
We're away from old Spiker and Sponge!'

One second later . . . slowly, insidiously, oh most
gently, the great peach started to lean forward and
steal into motion. The whole room began to tilt
over and all the furniture went sliding across the
floor, and crashed against the far wall. So did
James and the Ladybird and the Old-Green-Grasshopper and Miss Spider and the Earthworm, and
also the Centipede, who had just come slithering
quickly down the wall.

Fifteen

Outside in the garden, at that very moment, Aunt
Sponge and Aunt Spiker had just taken their places
at the front gate, each with a bunch of tickets in
her hand, and the first stream of early morning
sightseers was visible in the distance climbing up
the hill to view the peach.

'We shall make a fortune today,' Aunt Spiker
was saying. 'Just look at all those people!'

'I wonder what became of that horrid little boy
of ours last night,' Aunt Sponge said. 'He never did
come back in, did he?'

'He probably fell down in the dark and broke his
leg,' Aunt Spiker said.

'Or his neck, maybe,' Aunt Sponge said
hopefully.

'Just *wait* till I get my hands on him,' Aunt
Spiker said, waving her cane. 'He'll never want to

stay out all night again by the time *I've* finished with him. Good gracious me! What's that awful noise?'

Both women swung round to look.

The noise, of course, had been caused by the giant peach crashing through the fence that surrounded it, and now, gathering speed every second, it came rolling across the garden towards the place where Aunt Sponge and Aunt Spiker were standing.

They gaped. They screamed. They started to

244

run. They panicked. They both got in each other's way. They began pushing and jostling, and each one of them was thinking only about saving herself. Aunt Sponge, the fat one, tripped over a box that she'd brought along to keep the money in, and fell flat on her face. Aunt Spiker immediately tripped over Aunt Sponge and came down on top of her. They both lay on the ground, fighting and clawing and yelling and struggling frantically to get up again, but before they could do this, the mighty peach was upon them.

There was a crunch.

And then there was silence.

The peach rolled on. And behind it, Aunt Sponge and Aunt Spiker lay ironed out upon the grass as flat and thin and lifeless as a couple of paper dolls cut out of a picture book.

Sixteen

And now the peach had broken out of the garden and was over the edge of the hill, rolling and bouncing down the steep slope at a terrific pace. Faster and faster and faster it went, and the crowds of people who were climbing up the hill suddenly caught sight of this terrible monster plunging down upon them and they screamed and scattered to right and left as it went hurtling by.

At the bottom of the hill it charged across the

road, knocking over a telegraph pole and flattening two parked cars as it went by.

Then it rushed madly across about twenty fields, breaking down all the fences and hedges in its path. It went right through the middle of a herd of fine Jersey cows, and then through a flock of sheep, and then through a paddock full of horses, and then through a yard full of pigs, and soon the whole countryside was a seething mass of panic-stricken animals stampeding in all directions.

The peach was still going at a tremendous speed with no sign of slowing down, and about a mile farther on it came to a village.

Down the main street of the village it rolled, with people leaping frantically out of its path right and left, and at the end of the street it went crashing right through the wall of an enormous building and out the other side, leaving two gaping round holes in the brickwork.

This building happened to be a famous factory where they made chocolate, and almost at once a great river of warm melted chocolate came pouring out of the holes in the factory wall. A minute later, this brown sticky mess was flowing through every street in the village, oozing under the doors of houses and into people's shops and gardens. Children were wading in it up to their knees, and some were even trying to swim in it and all of them were sucking it into their mouths in great greedy gulps and shrieking with joy.

But the peach rushed on across the countryside – on and on and on, leaving a trail of destruction in

its wake. Cowsheds, stables, pigsties, barns, bunga-
lows, hayricks, anything that got in its way went
toppling over like a ninepin. An old man sitting
quietly beside a stream had his fishing rod whisked
out of his hands as it went dashing by, and a
woman called Daisy Entwistle was standing so close
to it as it passed that she had the skin taken off the
tip of her long nose.

Would it ever stop?

Why should it? A round object will always keep
on rolling as long as it is on a downhill slope, and
in this case the land sloped downhill all the way
until it reached the ocean – the same ocean that
James had begged his aunts to be allowed to visit
the day before.

Well, perhaps he was going to visit it now. The
peach was rushing closer and closer to it every
second, and closer also to the towering white cliffs
that came first.

These cliffs are the most famous in the whole of
England, and they are hundreds of feet high. Below
them, the sea is deep and cold and hungry. Many
ships have been swallowed up and lost for ever on
this part of the coast, and all the men who were in
them as well. The peach was now only a hundred
yards away from the cliff – now fifty – now twenty
– now ten – now five – and when it reached the
edge of the cliff it seemed to leap up into the sky
and hang there suspended for a few seconds, still
turning over and over in the air.

Then it began to fall . . .

Down . . .

Down . . .
Down . . .
Down . . .
Down . . .
SMACK! It hit the water with a colossal splash and sank like a stone.

But a few seconds later, up it came again, and this time, up it stayed, floating serenely upon the surface of the water.

Seventeen

At this moment, the scene inside the peach itself was one of indescribable chaos. James Henry Trotter was lying bruised and battered on the floor of the room amongst a tangled mass of Centipede and Earthworm and Spider and Ladybird and Glowworm and Old-Green-Grasshopper. In the whole history of the world, no travellers had ever had a more terrible journey than these unfortunate creatures. It had started out well, with much laughing and shouting, and for the first few seconds, as the peach had begun to roll slowly forward, nobody had minded being tumbled about a little bit. And when it went *BUMP!*, and the Centipede had shouted, '*That* was Aunt Sponge!' and then *BUMP!* again, and '*That* was Aunt Spiker!' there had been a tremendous burst of cheering all round.

But as soon as the peach rolled out of the garden

and began to go down the steep hill, rushing and plunging and bounding madly downward, then the whole thing became a nightmare. James found himself being flung up against the ceiling, then back on to the floor, then sideways against the wall, then up on to the ceiling again, and up and down and back and forth and round and round, and at the same time all the other creatures were flying through the air in every direction, and so were the chairs and the sofa, not to mention the forty-two boots belonging to the Centipede. Everything and all of them were being rattled around like peas inside an enormous rattle that was being rattled by a mad giant who refused to stop. To make it worse, something went wrong with the Glow-worm's lighting system, and the room was in pitchy darkness. There were screams and yells and curses and cries of pain, and everything kept going round and round, and once James made a frantic grab at some thick bars sticking out from the wall only to find that they were a couple of the Centipede's legs. 'Let go, you idiot!' shouted the Centipede, kicking himself free, and James was promptly flung across the room into the Old-Green-Grasshopper's horny lap. Twice he got tangled up in Miss Spider's legs (a horrid business), and towards the end, the poor Earthworm, who was cracking himself like a whip every time he flew through the air from one side of the room to the other, coiled himself around James's body in a panic and refused to unwind.

Oh, it was a frantic and terrible trip!

But it was all over now, and the room was
suddenly very still and quiet. Everybody was beginning slowly and painfully to disentangle himself
from everybody else.

'Let's have some light!' shouted the Centipede.

'Yes!' they cried. 'Light! Give us some light!'

'I'm *trying*,' answered the poor Glow-worm. 'I'm doing my best. Please be patient.'

They all waited in silence.

Then a faint greenish light began to glimmer out of the Glow-worm's tail, and this gradually became stronger and stronger until it was anyway enough to see by.

'*Some great journey!*' the Centipede said, limping across the room.

'I shall *never* be the same again,' murmured the Earthworm.

'Nor I,' the Ladybird said. 'It's taken *years* off my life.'

'But my dear friends!' cried the Old-Green-Grass-hopper, trying to be cheerful. 'We are *there!*'

'Where?' they asked. 'Where? Where is *there?*'

'I don't know,' the Old-Green-Grasshopper said. 'But I'll bet it's somewhere good.'

'We are probably at the bottom of a coal mine,' the Earthworm said gloomily. 'We certainly went down and down and down very suddenly at the last moment. I felt it in my stomach. I still feel it.'

'Perhaps we are in the middle of a beautiful country full of songs and music,' the Old-Green-Grasshopper said.

'Or near the seashore,' said James eagerly, 'with lots of other children down on the sand for me to play with!'

'Pardon me,' murmured the Ladybird, turning a trifle pale, 'but am I wrong in thinking that we seem to be bobbing up and down?'

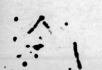

'*Bobbing* up and down!' they cried. 'What on earth do you mean?'

'You're still giddy from the journey,' the Old-Green-Grasshopper told her. 'You'll get over it in a minute. Is everybody ready to go upstairs now and take a look round?'

'Yes, yes!' they chorused. 'Come on! Let's go!'

'I *refuse* to show myself out of doors in my bare feet,' the Centipede said. 'I *have* to get my boots on again first.'

'For heaven's sake, let's not go through all that nonsense again,' the Earthworm said.

'Let's *all* lend the Centipede a hand and get it over with,' the Ladybird said. 'Come on.'

So they did, all except Miss Spider, who set about weaving a long rope-ladder that would reach from the floor up to a hole in the ceiling. The Old-Green-Grasshopper had wisely said that they must not risk going out of the side entrance when they didn't know where they were, but must first of all go up on to the top of the peach and have a look round.

So half an hour later, when the rope-ladder had been finished and hung, and the forty-second boot had been laced neatly on to the Centipede's forty-second foot, they were all ready to go out. Amidst mounting excitement and shouts of 'Here we go, boys! The Promised Land! I can't wait to see it!' the whole company climbed up the ladder one by one and disappeared into a dark soggy tunnel in the ceiling that went steeply, almost vertically, upward.

253

Eighteen

A minute later, they were out in the open, standing on the very top of the peach, near the stem, blinking their eyes in the strong sunlight and peering nervously around.

'What happened?'

'Where are we?'

'But this is *impossible!*'

'Unbelievable!'

'Terrible!'

'I *told* you we were bobbing up and down,' the Ladybird said.

'We're in the middle of the sea!' cried James.

And indeed they were. A strong current and a high wind had carried the peach so quickly away from the shore that already the land was out of sight. All around them lay the vast black ocean, deep and hungry. Little waves were bibbling against the sides of the peach.

'But how did it happen?' they cried. 'Where are the fields? Where are the woods? Where is England?' Nobody, not even James, could understand how in the world a thing like this could have come about.

'Ladies and gentlemen,' the Old-Green-Grasshopper said, trying very hard to keep the fear and disappointment out of his voice, 'I am afraid that we find ourselves in a rather awkward situation.'

'Awkward!' cried the Earthworm. 'My dear Old Grasshopper, we are finished! Every one of us is about to perish! I may be blind, you know, but that much I can see quite clearly.'

'Off with my boots!' shouted the Centipede. 'I cannot swim with my boots on!'

'I can't swim at all!' cried the Ladybird.

'Nor can I,' wailed the Glow-worm.

'Nor I!' said Miss Spider. 'None of us three girls can swim a single stroke.'

'But you won't *have* to swim,' said James calmly. 'We are floating beautifully. And sooner or later a ship is bound to come along and pick us up.'

They all stared at him in amazement.

'Are you quite sure that we are not sinking?' the Ladybird asked.

'Of course I'm sure,' answered James. 'Go and look for yourselves.'

They all ran over to the side of the peach and peered down at the water below.

'The boy is quite right,' the Old-Green-Grass-hopper said. 'We are floating beautifully. Now we must all sit down and keep perfectly calm. Everything will be all right in the end.'

'What absolute nonsense!' cried the Earthworm. 'Nothing is ever all right in the end, and well you know it!'

'Poor Earthworm,' the Ladybird said, whispering in James's ear. 'He loves to make everything into a disaster. He hates to be happy. He is only happy when he is gloomy. Now isn't that odd? But then, I suppose just *being* an Earthworm is enough to make a person pretty gloomy, don't you agree?'

'If this peach is not going to sink,' the Earthworm

was saying, 'and if we are not going to be drowned, then every one of us is going to *starve* to death instead. Do you realize that we haven't had a thing to eat since yesterday morning?'

'By golly, he's right!' cried the Centipede. 'For once, Earthworm is right!'

'Of course I'm right,' the Earthworm said. 'And we're not likely to find anything around here either. We shall get thinner and thinner and thirstier and thirstier, and we shall all die a slow and grisly death from starvation. I am dying already. I am slowly shrivelling up for want of food. Personally, I would rather drown.'

'But good heavens, you must be *blind!*' said James.

'You know very well I'm blind,' snapped the Earthworm. 'There's no need to rub it in.'

'I didn't mean that,' said James quickly. 'I'm sorry. But can't you *see* that – '

'See?' shouted the poor Earthworm. 'How can I see if I am blind?'

James took a deep, slow breath. 'Can't you *realize*,' he said patiently, 'that we have enough food here to last us for weeks and weeks?'

'Where?' they said. 'Where?'

'Why, the peach of course! Our whole ship is made of food!'

'Jumping Jehoshophat!' they cried. 'We never thought of that!'

'My dear James,' said the Old-Green-Grasshopper, laying a front leg affectionately on James's shoulder, 'I don't know what we'd do without you.

You are so clever. Ladies and gentlemen – we are saved again!'

'We are most certainly not!' said the Earthworm. 'You must be crazy! You can't eat the ship! It's the only thing that is keeping us up!'

'We shall starve if we don't!' said the Centipede.

'And we shall drown if we do!' cried the Earthworm.

'Oh dear, oh dear,' said the Old-Green-Grasshopper. 'Now we're worse off than before!'

'Couldn't we just eat a *little* bit of it?' asked Miss Spider. 'I am so dreadfully hungry.'

'You can eat all you want,' James answered. 'It would take us weeks and weeks to make any sort of a dent in this enormous peach. Surely you can see that?'

'Good heavens, he's right again!' cried the Old-Green-Grasshopper, clapping his hands. 'It would take weeks and weeks! Of course it would! But let's not go making a lot of holes all over the deck. I think we'd better simply scoop it out of that tunnel over there – the one that we've just come up by.'

'An excellent idea,' said the Ladybird.

'What are you looking so worried about, Earthworm?' the Centipede asked. 'What's the problem?'

'The problem is . . .' the Earthworm said, 'the problem is . . . well, the problem is that there is no problem!'

Everyone burst out laughing. 'Cheer up, Earthworm!' they said. 'Come and eat!' And they all went over to the tunnel entrance and began scooping out great chunks of juicy, golden-coloured peach flesh.

'Oh, marvellous!' said the Centipede, stuffing it into his mouth.

'*Dee*-licious!' said the Old-Green-Grasshopper.

'Just fabulous!' said the Glow-worm.

'Oh my!' said the Ladybird primly. 'What a heavenly taste!' She looked up at James, and she smiled, and James smiled back at her. They sat down on the deck together, both of them chewing away happily. 'You know, James,' the Ladybird said, 'up until this moment, I have never in my life tasted anything except those tiny little green flies that live on rosebushes. They have a perfectly delightful flavour. But this peach is even better.'

'Isn't it glorious!' Miss Spider said, coming over to join them. 'Personally, I had always thought that a big, juicy, caught-in-the-web bluebottle was the finest dinner in the world – until I tasted *this*.'

'*What* a flavour!' the Centipede cried. 'It's terrific! There's nothing like it! There never has been! And I should know because I personally have tasted all the finest foods in the world!' Whereupon, the Centipede, with his mouth full of peach and with juice running down all over his chin, suddenly burst into song:

'*I've eaten many strange and scrumptious dishes in my time,*
Like jellied gnats and dandyprats and earwigs cooked in slime,
And mice with rice – they're really nice
When roasted in their prime.
(But don't forget to sprinkle them with just a pinch of grime.)

'I've eaten fresh mudburgers by the greatest cooks there
are,
And scrambled dregs and stinkbugs' eggs and hornets
stewed in tar,
And pails of snails and lizards' tails,
And beetles by the jar.
(A beetle is improved by just a splash of vinegar.)

'I often eat boiled slobbages. They're grand when
served beside
Minced doodlebugs and curried slugs. And have you
ever tried
Mosquitoes' toes and wampfish roes
Most delicately fried?
(The only trouble is they disagree with my inside.)

'I'm mad for crispy wasp-stings on a piece of buttered
toast,
And pickled spines of porcupines. And then a gorgeous
roast
Of dragon's flesh, well hung, not fresh –
It costs a pound at most.
(And comes to you in barrels if you order it by post.)

'I crave the tasty tentacles of octopi for tea
I like hot-dogs, I LOVE hot-frogs, and surely you'll
agree
A plate of soil with engine oil's
A super recipe.
(I hardly need to mention that it's practically free.)

'*For dinner on my birthday shall I tell you what I
    chose:
Hot noodles made from poodles on a slice of garden
    hose –
And a rather smelly jelly
Made of armadillo's toes.
(The jelly is delicious, but you have to hold your nose.)*

'*Now comes,*' the Centipede declared, '*the burden
    of my speech:
These foods are rare beyond compare – some are right
    out of reach;
But there's no doubt I'd go without
A million plates of each
For one small mite,
One tiny bite,
Of this* FANTASTIC PEACH!'

  Everybody was feeling happy now. The sun was
shining brightly out of a soft blue sky and the day
was calm. The giant peach, with the sunlight glinting on its side, was like a massive golden ball
sailing upon a silver sea.

Nineteen

'Look!' cried the Centipede just as they were finish-
ing their meal. 'Look at that funny thin black
thing gliding through the water over there!'

They all swung round to look.

'There are two of them,' said Miss Spider.

'There are *lots* of them!' said the Ladybird.

'What are they?' asked the Earthworm, getting worried.

'They must be some kind of fish,' said the Old-Green-Grasshopper. 'Perhaps they have come along to say hello.'

'They are sharks!' cried the Earthworm. 'I'll bet you anything you like that they are sharks and they have come along to eat us up!'

'What absolute rot!' the Centipede said, but his voice seemed suddenly to have become a little shaky, and he wasn't laughing.

'I am *positive* they are sharks!' said the Earthworm. 'I just *know* they are sharks!'

And so, in actual fact, did everybody else, but they were too frightened to admit it.

There was a short silence. They all peered down anxiously at the sharks who were cruising slowly round and round the peach.

'Just assuming that they *are* sharks,' the Centipede said, 'there still can't possibly be any danger if we stay up here.'

But even as he spoke, one of those thin black fins suddenly changed direction and came cutting swiftly through the water right up to the side of the peach itself. The shark paused and stared up at the company with small evil eyes.

'Go away!' they shouted. 'Go away, you filthy beast!'

Slowly, almost lazily, the shark opened his mouth

(which was big enough to have swallowed a peram-
bulator) and made a lunge at the peach.

They all watched, aghast.

And now, as though at a signal from the leader,
all the other sharks came swimming in towards the
peach, and they clustered around it and began to
attack it furiously. There must have been twenty or
thirty of them at least, all pushing and fighting and
lashing their tails and churning the water into a
froth.

Panic and pandemonium broke out immediately
on top of the peach.

'Oh, we are finished now!' cried Miss Spider,
wringing her feet. 'They will eat up the whole
peach and then there'll be nothing left for us to
stand on and they'll start on us!'

'She is right!' shouted the Ladybird. 'We are lost
for ever!'

'Oh, I don't want to be eaten!' wailed the Earthworm. 'But they will take me first of all because I
am so fat and juicy and I have no bones!'

'Is there *nothing* we can do?' asked the Ladybird,
appealing to James. 'Surely *you* can think of a way
out of this.'

Suddenly they were all looking at James.

'Think!' begged Miss Spider. '*Think*, James,
think!'

'Come on,' said the Centipede. 'Come on, James. There *must* be *something* we can do.'

Their eyes waited upon him, tense, anxious, pathetically hopeful.

Twenty

'There *is something* that I believe we might try,' James Henry Trotter said slowly. 'I'm not saying it'll work . . .'

'Tell us!' cried the Earthworm. 'Tell us quick!'

'We'll try anything you say!' said the Centipede. 'But hurry, hurry, hurry!'

'Be quiet and let the boy speak!' said the Ladybird. 'Go on, James.'

They all moved a little closer to him. There was a longish pause.

'Go *on!*' they cried frantically. '*Go on!*'

And all the time while they were waiting they could hear the sharks threshing around in the water below them. It was enough to make anyone frantic.

'Come on, James,' the Ladybird said, coaxing him.

'I . . . I . . . I'm afraid it's no good after all,' James murmured, shaking his head. 'I'm terribly sorry. I forgot. We don't have any string. We'd need hundreds of yards of string to make this work.'

'What sort of string?' asked the Old-Green-Grass-hopper sharply.

'Any sort, just so long as it's strong.'

'But my dear boy, that's exactly what we do have! We've got all you want!'

'How? Where?'

'The Silkworm!' cried the Old-Green-Grass-hopper. 'Didn't you ever notice the Silkworm? She's still downstairs! She never moves! She just lies there sleeping all day long, but we can easily wake her up and make her spin!'

'And what about me, may I ask?' said Miss Spider. 'I can spin just as well as any Silkworm. What's more, *I* can spin patterns.'

'Can you make enough between you?' asked James.

'As much as you want.'

'And quickly?'

'Of course! Of course!'

'And would it be strong?'

'The strongest there is! It's as thick as your finger! But why? What are you going to do?'

'I'm going to lift this peach clear out of the water!' James announced firmly.

'You're mad!' cried the Earthworm.

'It's our only chance.'

'The boy's crazy.'

'He's joking.'

'Go on, James,' the Ladybird said gently. 'How are you going to do it?'

'Skyhooks, I suppose,' jeered the Centipede.

'Seagulls,' James answered calmly. 'The place is

full of them. Look up there!'

They all looked up and saw a great mass of seagulls wheeling round and round in the sky.

'I'm going to take a long silk string,' James went on, 'and I'm going to loop one end of it round a seagull's neck. And then I'm going to tie the other end to the stem of the peach.' He pointed to the peach stem, which was standing up like a short thick mast in the middle of the deck.

'Then I'm going to get another seagull and do the same thing again, then another and another – '

'Ridiculous!' they shouted.

'Absurd!'

'Poppycock!'

'Balderdash!'

'Madness!'

And the Old-Green-Grasshopper said, 'How can a few seagulls lift an enormous thing like this up into the air, and all of us as well? It would take hundreds . . . thousands . . .'

'There is no shortage of seagulls,' James answered. 'Look for yourself. We'll probably need four hundred, five hundred, six hundred . . . maybe even a thousand . . . I don't know . . . I shall simply go on hooking them up to the stem until we have enough to lift us. They'll be bound to lift us in the end. It's like balloons. You give someone enough balloons to hold, I mean *really* enough, then up he goes. And a seagull has far more lifting power than a balloon. If only we have the *time* to do it. If only we are not sunk first by those awful sharks . . .'

'You're absolutely off your head!' said the Earthworm.

'How on earth do you propose to get a loop of string round a seagull's neck? I suppose you're going to fly up there yourself and catch it!'

'The boy's dotty!' said the Centipede.

'Let him finish,' said the Ladybird. 'Go on, James. How *would* you do it?'

'With bait.'

'Bait! What sort of bait?'

'With a worm, of course. Seagulls love worms, didn't you know that? And luckily for us, we have here the biggest, fattest, pinkest, juiciest Earthworm in the world.'

'You can stop right there!' the Earthworm said sharply. 'That's quite enough!'

'Go on,' the others said, beginning to grow interested. 'Go on!'

'The seagulls have already spotted him,' James continued. 'That's why there are so many of them circling round. But they daren't come down to get him while all the rest of us are standing here. So this is what – '

'Stop!' cried the Earthworm. 'Stop, stop, stop! I won't have it! I refuse! I – I – I – I – '

'Be quiet!' said the Centipede. 'Mind your own business!'

'I *like* that!'

'My dear Earthworm, you're going to be eaten anyway, so what difference does it make whether it's sharks or seagulls?'

'I won't do it!'

'Why don't we hear what the plan is first?' said the Old-Green-Grasshopper.

'I don't give a hoot what the plan is!' cried the Earthworm. 'I am not going to be pecked to death by a bunch of seagulls!'

'You will be a martyr,' said the Centipede. 'I shall respect you for the rest of my life.'

'So will I,' said Miss Spider. 'And your name

will be in all the newspapers. Earthworm gives life to save friends . . .'

'But he won't *have* to give his life,' James told them. 'Now listen to me. This is what we'll do . . .'

Twenty-one

'Why, it's absolutely brilliant!' cried the Old-Green-Grasshopper when James had explained his plan.

'The boy's a genius!' the Centipede announced. 'Now I can keep my boots on after all.'

'Oh, I shall be pecked to death!' wailed the poor Earthworm.

'Of course you won't.'

'I will, I know I will! And I won't even be able to see them coming at me because I have no eyes!'

James went over and put an arm gently round the Earthworm's shoulders. 'I won't let them *touch* you,' he said. 'I promise I won't. But we've *got* to hurry! Look down there!'

There were more sharks than ever now around the peach. The water was boiling with them. There must have been ninety or a hundred at least. And to the travellers up on top, it certainly seemed as though the peach were sinking lower and lower into the water.

'Action stations!' James shouted. 'Jump to it!

There's not a moment to lose!' He was the captain
now, and everyone knew it. They would do whatever he told them.

'All hands below deck except Earthworm!' he
ordered.

'Yes, yes!' they said eagerly as they scuttled into
the tunnel entrance. 'Come on! Let's hurry!'

'And you – Centipede!' James shouted. 'Hop

downstairs and get that Silkworm to work at once! Tell her to spin as she's never spun before! Our lives depend upon it! And the same applies to you, Miss Spider! Hurry on down! Start spinning.'

Twenty-two

In a few minutes everything was ready.

It was very quiet now on the top of the peach. There was nobody in sight – nobody except the Earthworm.

One half of the Earthworm, looking like a great, thick, juicy, pink sausage, lay innocently in the sun for all the seagulls to see.

The other half of him was dangling down the tunnel.

James was crouching close beside the Earthworm in the tunnel entrance, just below the surface, waiting for the first seagull. He had a loop of silk string in his hands.

The Old-Green-Grasshopper and the Ladybird were further down the tunnel, holding on to the Earthworm's tail, ready to pull him quickly in out of danger as soon as James gave the word.

And far below, in the great stone of the peach, the Glow-worm was lighting up the room so that the two spinners, the Silkworm and Miss Spider, could see what they were doing. The Centipede was down there too, exhorting them both franti-cally to greater efforts, and every now and again James could hear his voice coming up faintly from the depths, shouting, 'Spin, Silkworm, spin, you great fat lazy brute! Faster, faster, or we'll throw you to the sharks!'

'Here comes the first seagull!' whispered James. 'Keep still now, Earthworm. Keep still. The rest of you get ready to pull.'

'Please don't let it spike me,' begged the Earthworm.

'I won't, I won't. Ssshh . . .'

Out of the corner of one eye, James watched the seagull as it came swooping down towards the Earthworm. And then suddenly it was so close that he could see its small black eyes and its curved beak, and the beak was open, ready to grab a nice piece of flesh out of the Earthworm's back.

'Pull!' shouted James.

The Old-Green-Grasshopper and the Ladybird gave the Earthworm's tail an enormous tug, and like magic the Earthworm disappeared into the tunnel. At the same time, up went James's hand and the seagull flew right into the loop of silk that he was holding out. The loop, which had been cleverly made, tightened just the right amount (but not too much) around its neck, and the seagull was captured.

'Hooray!' shouted the Old-Green-Grasshopper, peering out of the tunnel. 'Well done, James!'

Up flew the seagull with James paying out the silk string as it went. He gave it about fifty yards

273

and then tied the string to the stem of the peach.

'Next one!' he shouted, jumping back into the tunnel. 'Up you get again, Earthworm! Bring up some more silk, Centipede!'

'Oh, I don't like this at all,' wailed the Earthworm. 'It only just missed me! I even felt the wind on my back as it went swishing past!'

'Ssshh!' whispered James. 'Keep still! Here comes another one!'

So they did it again.

And again, and again, and again.

And the seagulls kept coming, and James caught them one after the other and tethered them to the peach stem.

'One hundred seagulls!' he shouted, wiping the sweat from his face.

'Keep going!' they cried. 'Keep going, James!'

'Two hundred seagulls!'

'Three hundred seagulls!'

'Four hundred seagulls!'

The sharks, as though sensing that they were in danger of losing their prey, were hurling themselves at the peach more furiously than ever, and the peach was sinking lower and lower still in the water.

'Five hundred seagulls!' James shouted.

'Silkworm says she's running out of silk!' yelled the Centipede from below. 'She says she can't keep it up much longer. Nor can Miss Spider!'

'Tell them they've *got* to!' James answered. 'They can't stop now!'

'We're lifting!' somebody shouted.

'No, we're not!'

'I felt it!'

'Put on another seagull, quick!'

'Quiet, everybody! Quiet! Here's one coming now!'

This was the five hundred and first seagull, and the moment that James caught it and tethered it to the stem with all the others, the whole enormous peach suddenly started rising up slowly out of the water.

'Look out! Here we go! Hold on, boys!'

But then it stopped.

And there it hung.

It hovered and swayed, but it went no higher.

The bottom of it was just touching the water. It was like a delicately balanced scale that needed only the tiniest push to tip it one way or the other.

'One more will do it!' shouted the Old-Green-Grasshopper, looking out of the tunnel. 'We're almost there!'

And now came the big moment. Quickly, the five hundred and second seagull was caught and harnessed to the peach-stem . . .

And then suddenly . . .

But slowly . . .

Majestically . . .

Like some fabulous golden balloon . . .

With all the seagulls straining at the strings above . . .

The giant peach rose up dripping out of the water and began climbing towards the heavens.

Twenty-three

In a flash, everybody was up on top.

'Oh, isn't it beautiful!' they cried.

'What a marvellous feeling!'

'Good-bye, sharks!'

'Oh, boy, this is the way to travel!'

Miss Spider, who was literally squealing with excitement, grabbed the Centipede by the waist and the two of them started dancing round and round the peach stem together. The Earthworm stood up on his tail and did a sort of wriggle of joy all by himself. The Old-Green-Grasshopper kept hopping higher and higher in the air. The Ladybird rushed over and shook James warmly by the hand. The Glow-worm, who at the best of times was a very shy and silent creature, sat glowing with pleasure near the tunnel entrance. Even the Silkworm, looking white and thin and completely exhausted, came creeping out of the tunnel to watch this miraculous ascent.

Up and up they went, and soon they were as high as the top of a church steeple above the ocean.

'I'm a bit worried about the peach,' James said to the others as soon as all the dancing and the shouting had stopped. 'I wonder how much damage those sharks have done to it underneath. It's quite impossible to tell from up here.'

'Why don't I go over the side and make an inspection?' Miss Spider said. 'It'll be no trouble at

all, I assure you.' And without waiting for an answer, she quickly produced a length of silk thread and attached the end of it to the peach stem. 'I'll be back in a jiffy,' she said, and then she walked calmly over to the edge of the peach and jumped off, paying out the thread behind her as she fell.

The others crowded anxiously around the place where she had gone over.

'Wouldn't it be dreadful if the thread broke,' the Ladybird said.

There was a rather long silence.

'Are you all right, Miss Spider?' shouted the Old-Green-Grasshopper.

'Yes, thank you!' her voice answered from below. 'I'm coming up now!' And up she came, climbing foot over foot up the silk thread, and at the same time tucking the thread back cleverly into her body as she climbed past it.

'Is it *awful*?' they asked her. 'Is it all eaten away? Are there great holes in it everywhere?'

Miss Spider clambered back on to the deck with a pleased but also a rather puzzled look on her face. 'You won't believe this,' she said, 'but actually there's hardly any damage down there at all! The peach is almost untouched! There are just a few tiny pieces out of it here and there, but nothing more.'

'You must be mistaken,' James told her.

'Of course she's mistaken!' the Centipede said.

'I promise you I'm not,' Miss Spider answered.

'But there were hundreds of sharks around us!'

'They churned the water into a froth!'

'We saw their great mouths opening and shutting!'

'I don't care what you saw,' Miss Spider answered. 'They certainly didn't do much damage to the peach.'

'Then why did we start sinking?' the Centipede asked.

'Perhaps we *didn't* start sinking,' the Old-Green-Grasshopper suggested. 'Perhaps we were all so frightened that we simply imagined it.'

This, in point of fact, was closer to the truth than any of them knew. A shark, you see, has an extremely long sharp nose, and its mouth is set very awkwardly underneath its face and a long way back. This makes it more or less impossible for it to get its teeth into a vast smooth curving surface such as the side of a peach. Even if the creature turns on to its back it still can't do it, because the nose always gets in the way. If you have ever seen a small dog trying to get its teeth into an enormous ball, then you will be able to imagine roughly how it was with the sharks and the peach.

'It must have been some kind of magic,' the Ladybird said. 'The holes must have healed up by themselves.'

'Oh, look! There's a ship below us!' shouted James.

Everybody rushed to the side and peered over. None of them had ever seen a ship before.

'It looks like a big one.'

'It's got three funnels.'

'You can even see the people on the decks!'

'Let's wave to them. Do you think they can see *us*?'

Neither James nor any of the others knew it, but the ship that was now passing beneath them was actually the *Queen Mary* sailing out of the English Channel on her way to America. And on the bridge of the *Queen Mary*, the astonished Captain was standing with a group of his officers, all of them gaping at the great round ball hovering overhead.

'I don't like it,' the Captain said.

'Nor do I,' said the First Officer.

'Do you think it's following us?' said the Second Officer.

'I tell you I don't like it,' muttered the Captain.

'It could be dangerous,' the First Officer said.

'That's it!' cried the Captain. 'It's a secret weapon! Holy cats! Send a message to the Queen at once! The country must be warned! And give me my telescope.'

The First Officer handed the telescope to the Captain. The Captain put it to his eye.

'There's birds everywhere!' he cried. 'The whole sky is teeming with birds! What in the world are *they* doing? And wait! Wait a second! There are *people* on it! I can see them moving! There's a – a – do I have this darned thing focused right? It looks like a little boy in short trousers! Yes, I can distinctly see a little boy in short trousers standing up there! And there's a – there's a – there's a – a – a – a sort of *giant ladybird*!'

'Now just a minute, Captain!' the First Officer said.

'And a *colossal green grasshopper*!'

'Captain!' the First Officer said sharply. 'Captain, please!'

'And a *mammoth spider*!'

'Oh dear, he's been at the whisky again,' whispered the Second Officer.

'And an *enormous – a simply enormous centipede*!' screamed the Captain.

'Call the Ship's Doctor,' the First Officer said. 'Our Captain is not well.'

A moment later, the great round ball disappeared into a cloud, and the people on the ship never saw it again.

Twenty-four

But up on the peach itself, everyone was still happy and excited.

'I wonder where we'll finish up this time,' the Earthworm said.

'Who cares?' they answered. 'Seagulls always go back to the land sooner or later.'

Up and up they went, high above the highest clouds, the peach swaying gently from side to side as it floated along.

'Wouldn't this be a perfect time for a little music?' the Ladybird asked. 'How about it, Old Grasshopper?'

'With pleasure, dear lady,' the Old-Green-Grasshopper answered, bowing from the waist.

'Oh, hooray! He's going to play for us!' they cried, and immediately the whole company sat themselves down in a circle around the Old Green Musician – and the concert began.

From the moment that the first note was struck, the audience became completely spellbound. And as for James, never had he heard such beautiful music as this! In the garden at home on summer evenings, he had listened many times to the sound of grasshoppers chirping in the grass, and he had always liked the noise that they made. But this was a different kind of noise altogether. This was real music – chords, harmonies, tunes, and all the rest of it.

And what a wonderful instrument the Old-Green-

Grasshopper was playing upon. It was like a violin! It was almost exactly as though he were playing upon a violin!

The bow of the violin, the part that moved, was his back leg. The strings of the violin, the part that made the sound, was the edge of his wing.

He was using only the top of his back leg (the thigh), and he was stroking this up and down against the edge of his wing with incredible skill, sometimes slowly, sometimes fast, but always with the same easy flowing action. It was precisely the way a clever violinist would have used his bow; and the music came pouring out and filled the whole blue sky around them with magic melodies.

When the first part was finished, everyone clapped madly, and Miss Spider stood up and shouted, 'Bravo! Encore! Give us some more!'

'Did you like that, James?' the Old-Green-Grasshopper asked, smiling at the small boy.

'Oh, I loved it!' James answered. 'It was beautiful! It was as though you had a real violin in your hands!'

'A *real* violin!' the Old-Green-Grasshopper cried. 'Good heavens, I like that! My dear boy, I *am* a real violin! It is a part of my own body!'

'But do *all* grasshoppers play their music on violins, the same way as you do?' James asked him.

'No,' he answered, 'not all. If you want to know, I happen to be a "short-horned" grasshopper. I have two short feelers coming out of my head. Can you see them? There they are. They are quite short, aren't they? That's why they call me a "short-horn". And we "short-horns" are the only ones who play our music in the violin style, using a bow. My "long-horned" relatives, the ones who have long curvy feelers coming out of their heads, make their music simply by rubbing the edges of their two top wings together. They are not violin-ists, they are wing-rubbers. And a rather inferior noise these wing-rubbers produce, too, if I may say so. It sounds more like a banjo than a fiddle.'

'How fascinating this all is!' cried James. 'And to think that up until now I had never even *wondered* how a grasshopper made his sounds.'

'My dear young fellow,' the Old-Green-Grass-hopper said gently, 'there are a whole lot of things in this world of ours that you haven't started won-dering about yet. Where, for example, do you think that I keep my ears?'

'Your ears? Why, in your head, of course.'

Everyone burst out laughing.

'You mean you don't even know *that*?' cried the Centipede.

'Try again,' said the Old-Green-Grasshopper, smiling at James.

'You can't possibly keep them anywhere else?'

'Oh, can't I?'

'Well – I give up. Where *do* you keep them?'

'Right here,' the Old-Green-Grasshopper said. 'One on each side of my tummy.'

'It's not true!'

'Of course it's true. What's so peculiar about that? You ought to see where my cousins the crick-ets and the katydids keep theirs.'

'Where do they keep them?'

'In their legs. One in each front leg, just below the knee.'

'You mean you didn't know that either?' the Centipede said scornfully.

'You're joking,' James said. 'Nobody could possibly have his ears in his legs.'

'Why not?'

'Because . . . because it's ridiculous, that's why.'

'You know what I think is ridiculous?' the Centipede said, grinning away as usual. 'I don't mean to be rude, but *I* think it is ridiculous to have ears on the sides of one's head. It certainly *looks* ridiculous. You ought to take a peek in the mirror some day and see for yourself.'

'Pest!' cried the Earthworm. 'Why must you always be so rude and rambunctious to everyone? You ought to apologize to James at once.'

Twenty-five

James didn't want the Earthworm and the Centipede to get into another argument, so he said quickly to the Earthworm, 'Tell me, do *you* play any kind of music?'

'No, but I do *other* things, some of which are really quite *extraordinary*,' the Earthworm said, brightening.

'Such as what?' asked James.

286

'Well,' the Earthworm said. 'Next time you stand in a field or in a garden and look around you, then just remember this: that every grain of soil upon the surface of the land, every tiny little bit of soil that you can see has actually passed through the body of an Earthworm during the last few years! Isn't that wonderful?'

'It's not possible!' said James.

'My dear boy, it's a fact.'

'You mean you actually *swallow* soil?'

'Like mad,' the Earthworm said proudly. '*In* one end and *out* the other.'

'But what's the point?'

'What do you mean, what's the point?'

'Why do you do it?'

'We do it for the farmers. It makes the soil nice and light and crumbly so that things will grow well in it. If you really want to know, the farmers couldn't do without us. We are essential. We are vital. So it is only natural that the farmer should love us. He loves us even more, I believe, than he loves the Ladybird.'

'The Ladybird!' said James, turning to look at her. 'Do they love you, too?'

'I am told that they do,' the Ladybird answered modestly, blushing all over. 'In fact, I understand that in some places the farmers love us so much that they go out and buy live Ladybirds by the sackful and take them home and set them free in their fields. They are very pleased when they have lots of Ladybirds in their fields.'

'But why?' James asked.

'Because we gobble up all the nasty little insects that are gobbling up all the farmer's crops. It helps enormously, and we ourselves don't charge a penny for our services.'

'I think you're wonderful,' James told her. 'Can I ask you one special question?'

'Please do.'

'Well, is it really true that I can tell how old a Ladybird is by counting her spots?'

'Oh no, that's just a children's story,' the Ladybird said. 'We never change our spots. Some of us, of course, are born with more spots than others, but we never change them. The number of spots that a Ladybird has is simply a way of showing which branch of the family she belongs to. I, for example, as you can see for yourself, am a Nine-Spotted Ladybird. I am very lucky. It is a fine thing to be.'

'It is, indeed,' said James, gazing at the beautiful scarlet shell with the nine black spots on it.

'On the other hand,' the Ladybird went on, 'some of my less fortunate relatives have no more than two spots altogether on their shells! Can you imagine that? They are called Two-Spotted Ladybirds, and very common and ill-mannered they are, I regret to say. And then, of course, you have the Five-Spotted Ladybirds as well. They are much nicer than the Two-Spotted ones, although I myself find them a trifle too saucy for my taste.'

'But they are all of them loved?' said James.

'Yes,' the Ladybird answered quietly. 'They are all of them loved.'

'It seems that almost *everyone* around here is loved!' said James. 'How nice this is!'

'Not me!' cried the Centipede happily. 'I am a pest and I'm proud of it! Oh, I am such a shocking dreadful pest!'

'Hear, hear,' the Earthworm said.

'But what about you, Miss Spider?' asked James. 'Aren't you also much loved in the world?'

'Alas, no,' Miss Spider answered, sighing long and loud. 'I am not loved at all. And yet I do nothing but good. All day long I catch flies and mosquitoes in my webs. I am a decent person.'

'I know you are,' said James.

'It is very unfair the way we Spiders are treated,' Miss Spider went on. 'Why, only last week your own horrible Aunt Sponge flushed my poor dear father down the plug-hole in the bathtub.'

'Oh, how awful!' cried James.

'I watched the whole thing from a corner up in the ceiling,' Miss Spider murmured. 'It was ghastly.

We never saw him again.' A large tear rolled down
her cheek and fell with a splash on the floor.

'But is it not very unlucky to kill a spider?'
James inquired, looking around at the others.

'Of course it's unlucky to kill a spider!' shouted
the Centipede. 'It's about the unluckiest thing
anyone can do. Look what happened to Aunt
Sponge after she'd done that! *Bump!* We all felt it,
didn't we, as the peach went over her? Oh, what a
lovely bump that must have been for you, Miss
Spider!'

'It was very satisfactory,' Miss Spider answered.
Will you sing us a song about it, please?'

So the Centipede did.

> '*Aunt Sponge was terrifically fat,*
> *And tremendously flabby at that.*
> *Her tummy and waist*
> *Were as soggy as paste –*
> *It was worse on the place where she sat!*

So she said, "I must make myself flat.
I must make myself sleek as a cat.
I shall do without dinner
To make myself thinner."
But along came the peach!
Oh, the beautiful peach!
And made her far thinner than that!'

'That was very nice,' Miss Spider said. 'Now sing one about Aunt Spiker.'

'With pleasure,' the Centipede answered, grinning:

'Aunt Spiker was thin as a wire,
And dry as a bone, only drier.
She was so long and thin
If you carried her in
You could use her for poking the fire!

'"I must do something quickly," she frowned.
'I want FAT. I want pound upon pound!
I must eat lots and lots
Of marshmallows and chocs
Till I start bulging out all around."

'"Ah, yes," she announced, "I have sworn
That I'll alter my figure by dawn!"
Cried the peach with a snigger,
"I'LL alter your figure — "
And ironed her out on the lawn!'

Everybody clapped and called out for more songs from the Centipede, who at once launched into his favourite song of all:

'*Once upon a time*
When pigs were swine
And monkeys chewed tobacco
And hens took snuff
To make themselves tough
And the ducks said quack-quack-quacko,
And porcupines
Drank fiery wines
And goats ate tapioca
And Old Mother Hubbard
Got stuck in the c — '

'Look out, Centipede!' cried James. 'Look out!'

Twenty-six

The Centipede, who had begun dancing wildly round the deck during this song, had suddenly gone too close to the downward curving edge of the peach, and for three awful seconds he had stood teetering on the brink, swinging his legs frantically in circles in an effort to stop himself from falling over backward into space. But before anyone could reach him – down he went! He gave a shriek of terror as he fell, and the others, rushing to the side and peering over, saw his poor long body tumbling over and over through the air, getting smaller and smaller until it was out of sight.

'Silkworm!' yelled James. 'Quick! Start spinning!'

The Silkworm sighed, for she was still very tired from spinning all that silk for the seagulls, but she did as she was told.

'I'm going down after him!' cried James, grabbing the silk string as it started coming out of the Silkworm and tying the end of it around his waist. 'The rest of you hold on to Silkworm so I don't pull her over with me, and later on, if you feel three tugs on the string, start hauling me up again!'

He jumped, and he went tumbling down after the Centipede, down, down, down towards the sea below, and you can imagine how quickly the Silkworm had to spin to keep up with the speed of his fall.

'We'll never see either of them again!' cried the Ladybird. 'Oh, dear! Oh dear! Just when we were all so happy, too!'

Miss Spider, the Glow-worm, and the Ladybird all began to cry. So did the Earthworm. 'I don't care a bit about the Centipede,' the Earthworm sobbed. 'But I really did love that little boy.'

Very softly, the Old-Green-Grasshopper started to play the Funeral March on his violin, and by the time he had finished, everyone, including himself, was in a flood of tears.

Suddenly, there came three sharp tugs on the

rope. 'Pull!' shouted the Old-Green-Grasshopper.
'Everyone get behind me and pull!'

There was about a mile of string to be hauled in,
but they all worked like mad, and in the end, over
the side of the peach, there appeared a dripping-
wet James with a dripping-wet Centipede clinging
to him tightly with all forty-two of his legs.

'He saved me!' gasped the Centipede. 'He swam
around in the middle of the Atlantic Ocean until
he found me!'

'My dear boy,' the Old-Green-Grasshopper said, patting James on the back. 'I do congratulate you.'

'My boots!' cried the Centipede. 'Just look at my precious boots! They are ruined by the water!'

'Be quiet!' the Earthworm said. 'You are lucky to be alive.'

'Are we still going up and up?' asked James.

'We certainly are,' answered the Old-Green-Grasshopper. 'And it's beginning to get dark.'

'I know. It'll soon be night.'

'Why don't we all go down below and keep warm until tomorrow morning?' Miss Spider suggested.

'No,' the Old-Green-Grasshopper said. 'I think that would be very unwise. It will be safer if we all stay up here through the night and keep watch. Then, if anything happens, we shall anyway be ready for it.'

Twenty-seven

James Henry Trotter and his companions crouched close together on top of the peach as the night began closing in around them. Clouds like mountains towered high above their heads on all sides, mysterious, menacing, overwhelming. Gradually it grew darker and darker, and then a pale three-quarter moon came up over the tops of the clouds and cast an eerie light over the whole scene. The giant peach swayed gently from side to side as it floated along, and the hundreds of silky white strings going upward from its stem were beautiful in the moonlight. So also was the great flock of seagulls overhead.

There was not a sound anywhere. Travelling upon the peach was not in the least like travelling in an aeroplane. The aeroplane comes clattering and roaring through the sky, and whatever might be lurking secretly up there in the great cloud-mountains goes running for cover at its approach. That is why people who travel in aeroplanes never see anything.

But the peach ... ah, yes ... the peach was a soft, stealthy traveller, making no noise at all as it floated along. And several times during that long silent night ride high up over the middle of the ocean in the moonlight, James and his friends saw

things that no one had ever seen before.

Once, as they drifted silently past a massive white cloud, they saw on the top of it a group of strange, tall, wispy-looking things that were about twice the height of ordinary men. They were not easy to see at first because they were almost as white as the cloud itself, but as the peach sailed closer, it became obvious that these 'things' were actually living creatures – tall, wispy, wraithlike, shadowy, white creatures who looked as though they were made out of a mixture of cotton-wool and candyfloss and thin white hairs.

'Ooooooooooooooh!' the Ladybird said. 'I don't like this at all!'

'Ssshh!' James whispered back. 'Don't let them hear you! They must be Cloud-Men!'

'*Cloud-Men!*' they murmured, huddling closer together for comfort. 'Oh dear, oh dear!'

'I'm glad I'm blind and can't see them,' the Earthworm said, 'or I would probably scream.'

'I hope they don't turn round and see *us*,' Miss Spider stammered.

'Do you think they would eat us?' the Earthworm asked.

'They would eat *you*,' the Centipede answered, grinning. 'They would cut you up like a salami and eat you in thin slices.'

The poor Earthworm began to quiver all over with fright.

'But what are they *doing*?' the Old-Green-Grasshopper whispered.

'I don't know,' James answered softly. 'Let's watch and see.'

The Cloud-Men were all standing in a group, and they were doing something peculiar with their hands. First, they would reach out (all of them at once) and grab handfuls of cloud. Then they would roll these handfuls of cloud in their fingers until they turned into what looked like large white marbles. Then they would toss the marbles to one side and quickly grab more bits of cloud and start over again.

It was all very silent and mysterious. The pile of marbles beside them kept growing larger and larger. Soon there was a truckload of them there at least.

'They must be absolutely mad!' the Centipede said. 'There's nothing to be afraid of here!'

'Be quiet, you pest!' the Earthworm whispered. 'We shall *all* be eaten if they see us!'

But the Cloud-Men were much too busy with what they were doing to have noticed the great peach floating silently up behind them.

Then the watchers on the peach saw one of the Cloud-Men raising his long wispy arms above his head and they heard him shouting, 'All right, boys! That's enough! Get the shovels!' And all the other

Cloud-Men immediately let out a strange high-pitched whoop of joy and started jumping up and down and waving their arms in the air. Then they picked up enormous shovels and rushed over to the pile of marbles and began shovelling them as fast as they could over the side of the cloud, into space. '*Down they go!*' they chanted as they worked.

'Down they go!
Hail and snow!
Freezes and sneezes and noses will blow!'

'It's *hailstones*!' whispered James excitedly. 'They've been making hailstones and now they are showering them down on to the people in the world below!'

'Hailstones?' the Centipede said. 'That's ridiculous! This is summertime. You don't have hailstones in summertime.'

'They are practising for the winter,' James told him.

'I don't believe it!' shouted the Centipede, raising his voice.

'Ssshh!' the others whispered. And James said softly, 'For heaven's sake, Centipede, don't make so much noise.'

The Centipede roared with laughter. 'Those imbeciles couldn't hear anything!' he cried. 'They're deaf as doorknobs! You watch!' And before anyone could stop him, he had cupped his front feet to his mouth and was yelling at the Cloud-Men as loud as he could. 'Idiots!' he yelled. 'Nincompoops!

Half-wits! Blunderheads! Asses! What on earth do you think you're doing over there!'

The effect was immediate. The Cloud-Men jumped round as if they had been stung by wasps. And when they saw the great golden peach floating past them not fifty yards away in the sky, they gave a yelp of surprise and dropped their shovels to the ground. And there they stood with the moon-light streaming down all over them, absolutely motionless, like a group of tall white hairy statues, staring and staring at the gigantic fruit as it went sailing by.

The passengers on the peach (all except the Centipede) sat frozen with terror, looking back at the Cloud-Men and wondering what was going to happen next.

'Now you've done it, you loathsome pest!' whispered the Earthworm to the Centipede.

'I'm not frightened of *them*!' shouted the Centipede, and to show everybody once again that he wasn't, he stood up to his full height and started dancing about and making insulting signs at the Cloud-Men with all forty-two of his legs.

This evidently infuriated the Cloud-Men beyond belief. All at once, they spun round and grabbed great handfuls of hailstones and rushed to the edge of the cloud and started throwing them at the peach, shrieking with fury all the time.

'Look out!' cried James. 'Quick! Lie down! Lie flat on the deck!'

It was lucky they did! A large hailstone can hurt you as much as a rock or a lump of lead if it is thrown hard enough – and my goodness, how those Cloud-Men could throw! The hailstones came whizzing through the air like bullets from a machine-gun, and James could hear them smashing against the sides of the peach and burying themselves in the peach flesh with horrible squelching noises – *plop! plop! plop! plop!* And then *ping! ping! ping!* as they bounced off the poor Ladybird's shell because she couldn't lie as flat as the others. And then *crack!* as one of them hit the Centipede right on the nose and *crack!* again as another one hit him somewhere else.

'Ow!' he cried. 'Ow! Stop! Stop! Stop!'

But the Cloud-Men had no intention of stopping. James could see them rushing about on the cloud like a lot of huge hairy ghosts, picking up hailstones from the pile, dashing to the edge of the cloud, hurling the hailstones at the peach, dashing back again to get more, and then, when the pile of stones was all gone, they simply grabbed handfuls of cloud and made as many more as they wanted, and much bigger ones now, some of them as large as cannon balls.

'Quickly!' cried James. 'Down the tunnel or we'll all be wiped out!'

There was a rush for the tunnel entrance, and half a minute later everybody was safely downstairs inside the stone of the peach, trembling with fright and listening to the noise of the hailstones as they came crashing against the side of the peach.

'I'm a wreck!' groaned the Centipede. 'I am

wounded all over!'

'It serves you right,' said the Earthworm.

'Would somebody kindly look and see if my shell is cracked?' the Ladybird said.

'Give us some light!' shouted the Old-Green-Grasshopper.

'I can't!' wailed the Glow-worm. 'They've broken my bulb!'

'Then put in another one!' the Centipede said.

'Be quiet a moment,' said James. 'Listen! I do believe they're not hitting us any more!'

They all stopped talking and listened. Yes – the noise had ceased. The hailstones were no longer smashing against the peach.

'We've left them behind!'

'The seagulls must have pulled us away out of danger.'

'Hooray! Let's go up and see!'

Cautiously, with James going first, they all climbed back up the tunnel. James poked his head out and looked around. 'It's all clear!' he called. 'I can't see them anywhere!'

Twenty-eight

One by one, the travellers came out again on to the top of the peach and gazed carefully around. The moon was still shining as brightly as ever, and there were still plenty of huge shimmering cloud-mountains on all sides. But there were no Cloud-Men in sight now.

'The peach is leaking!' shouted the Old-Green-Grasshopper, peering over the side. 'It's full of holes and the juice is dripping out everywhere!'

'*That* does it!' cried the Earthworm. 'If the peach is leaking then we shall surely sink!'

'Don't be an ass!' the Centipede told him. 'We're not in the water now!'

'Oh, look!' shouted the Ladybird. 'Look, look, look! Over there!'

Everybody swung round to look.

In the distance and directly ahead of them, they now saw a most extraordinary sight. It was a kind of arch, a colossal curvy-shaped thing that reached high up into the sky and came down again at both ends. The ends were resting upon a huge flat cloud that was as big as a desert.

'Now what in the world is that?' asked James.

'It's a bridge!'

'It's an enormous hoop cut in half!'

'It's a giant horseshoe standing upside down!'

'Stop me if I'm wrong,' murmured the Centipede, going white in the face, 'but might those not be Cloud-Men climbing all over it?'

There was a dreadful silence. The peach floated closer and closer.

'They *are* Cloud-Men!'

'There are hundreds of them!'

'Thousands!'

'Millions!'

'I don't want to hear about it!' shrieked the poor

blind Earthworm. 'I'd rather be on the end of a fish hook and used as bait than come up against those terrible creatures again!'

'I'd rather be fried alive and eaten by a Mexican!' wailed the Old-Green-Grasshopper.

'Please keep quiet,' whispered James. 'It's our only hope.'

They crouched very still on top of the peach, staring at the Cloud-Men. The whole surface of the cloud was literally *swarming* with them, and there were hundreds more up above climbing about on that monstrous crazy arch.

'But what is that thing?' whispered the Ladybird. 'And what are they *doing* to it?'

'I don't care what they're doing to it!' the Centipede said, scuttling over to the tunnel entrance. 'I'm not staying up here! Good-bye!'

But the rest of them were too frightened or too hypnotized by the whole affair to make a move.

'Do you know what?' James whispered.

'*What?*' they said. '*What?*'

'That enormous arch — they seem to be *painting* it! They've got pots of paint and big brushes! You look!'

And he was quite right. The travellers were close enough now to see that this was exactly what the Cloud-Men were doing. They all had huge brushes in their hands and they were splashing the paint on to the great curvy arch in a frenzy of speed, so fast, in fact, that in a few minutes the whole of the arch became covered with the most glorious colours — reds,

305

blues, greens, yellows, and purples.

'It's a rainbow!' everyone said at once. 'They are making a rainbow!'

'Oh, isn't it beautiful!'

'Just look at those colours!'

'Centipede!' they shouted. 'You *must* come up and see this!' They were so enthralled by the beauty and brilliance of the rainbow that they forgot to keep their voices low any longer. The Centipede poked his head cautiously out of the tunnel entrance.

'Well, well, well,' he said. 'I've *always* wondered how those things were made. But why all the ropes? What are they doing with those ropes?'

'Good heavens, they are pushing it off the cloud!' cried James. 'There it goes! They are lowering it down to the earth with ropes!'

'And I'll tell you something else,' the Centipede said sharply. 'If I'm not greatly mistaken, we ourselves are going to bump right into it!'

'Bless my soul, he's right!' the Old-Green-Grasshopper exclaimed.

The rainbow was now dangling in the air below the cloud. The peach was also just below the level of the cloud, and it was heading directly towards the rainbow, travelling rather fast.

'We are lost!' Miss Spider cried, wringing her feet again. 'The end has come!'

'I can't stand it!' wailed the Earthworm. 'Tell me what's happening!'

'We're going to miss it!' shouted the Ladybird.

'No, we're not!'

'Yes, we are!'

'Yes! – Yes! – No! – Oh, my heavens!'

'Hold on, everybody!' James called out, and suddenly there was a tremendous thud as the peach went crashing into the top of the rainbow. This

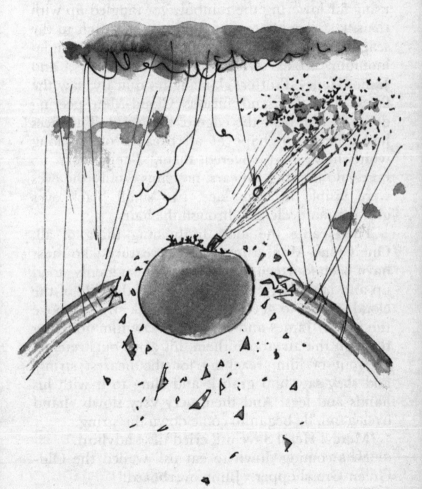

was followed by an awful splintering noise as the enormous rainbow snapped right across the middle and became two separate pieces.

The next thing that happened was extremely unfortunate. The ropes that the Cloud-Men had been using for lowering the rainbow got tangled up with the silk strings that went up from the peach to the seagulls! The peach was trapped! Panic and pandemonium broke out among the travellers, and James Henry Trotter, glancing up quickly, saw the faces of a thousand furious Cloud-Men peering down at him over the edge of the cloud. The faces had almost no shape at all because of the long white hairs that covered them. There were no noses, no mouths, no ears, no chins – only the eyes were visible in each face, two small black eyes glinting malevolently through the hairs.

Then came the most frightening thing of all. One Cloud-Man, a huge hairy creature who must have been fourteen feet tall at least, suddenly stood up and made a tremendous leap off the side of the cloud, trying to get to one of the silk strings above the peach. James and his friends saw him go flying through the air above them, his arms outstretched in front of him, reaching for the nearest string, and they saw him grab it and cling to it with his hands and legs. And then, very very slowly, hand over hand, he began to come down the string.

'Mercy! Help! Save us!' cried the Ladybird.

'He's coming down to eat us!' wailed the Old-Green-Grasshopper. 'Jump overboard!'

'Then eat the Earthworm first!' shouted the Cen-

tipede. 'It's no good eating me, I'm full of bones like a kipper!'

'Centipede!' yelled James. 'Quickly! Bite through that string, the one he's coming down on!'

The Centipede rushed over to the stem of the peach and took the silk string in his teeth and bit through it with one snap of his jaws. Immediately, far above them, a single seagull was seen to come away from the rest of the flock and go flying off with a long string trailing from its neck. And clinging desperately to the end of the string, shouting and cursing with fury, was the huge hairy Cloud-Man. Up and up he went, swinging across the moonlit sky, and James Henry Trotter, watching him with delight, said, 'My goodness, he must weigh almost nothing at all for one seagull to be able to pull him up like that! He must be all hair and air!'

The rest of the Cloud-Men were so flabbergasted at seeing one of their company carried away in this manner that they let go the ropes they were holding and then of course down went the rainbow, both halves of it together, tumbling towards the earth below. This freed the peach, which at once began sailing away from that terrible cloud.

But the travellers were not in the clear yet. The infuriated Cloud-Men jumped up and ran after them along the cloud, pelting them mercilessly with all sorts of hard and horrible objects. Empty paint buckets, paint brushes, stepladders, stools, saucepans, frying-pans, rotten eggs, dead rats, bottles of hair-oil – anything those brutes could lay their hands on came raining down upon the peach. One Cloud-Man, taking very careful aim, tipped a gallon of thick purple paint over the edge of the cloud right on to the Centipede himself.

The Centipede screamed with anger. 'My legs!' he cried. 'They are all sticking together! I can't walk! And my eyelids won't open! I can't see! And my boots! My boots are ruined!'

But for the moment everyone was far too busy dodging the things that the Cloud-Men were throwing to pay any attention to the Centipede.

'The paint is drying!' he moaned. 'It's going hard! I can't move my legs! I can't move anything!'

'You can still move your mouth,' the Earthworm said. 'And that is a great pity.'

'James!' bawled the Centipede. 'Please help me! Wash off this paint! Scrape it off! Anything!'

Twenty-nine

It seemed like a long time before the seagulls were able to pull the peach away from that horrible rainbow-cloud. But they managed it at last, and then everybody gathered around the wretched Centipede and began arguing about the best way to get the paint off his body.

He really did look a sight. He was purple all over, and now that the paint was beginning to dry and harden, he was forced to sit very stiff and upright, as though he were encased in cement. And all forty-two of his legs were sticking out straight in front of him, like rods. He tried to say something, but his lips wouldn't move. All he could do now was to make gurgling noises in his throat.

The Old-Green-Grasshopper reached out and touched him carefully on the stomach. 'But how could it possibly have dried so quickly?' he asked.

'It's rainbow-paint,' James answered. 'Rainbow-paint dries very quick and very hard.'

'I detest paint,' Miss Spider announced. 'It frightens me. It reminds me of Aunt Spiker – the *late* Aunt Spiker, I mean – because the last time she painted her kitchen ceiling my poor darling grandmother stepped into it by mistake when it was still wet, and there she stuck. And all through the night we could hear her calling to us, saying "Help! help! help!" and it was heartbreaking to listen to her. But what could we do? Not a thing until the next day when the paint had dried, and then of course we all rushed over to her and calmed her down and gave her some food. Believe it or not, she lived for six months like that, upside down on the ceiling with her legs stuck permanently in the paint. She really did. We fed her every day. We brought her fresh flies straight from the web. But then on the twenty-sixth of April last, Aunt Sponge – the *late* Aunt Sponge, I mean – happened to glance up at the ceiling, and she spotted her. "A spider!" she cried. "A disgusting spider! Quick! Fetch me the mop with the long handle!" And then – Oh, it was so awful I can't bear to think of it . . .' Miss Spider wiped away a tear and looked sadly at the Centipede. 'You poor thing,' she murmured. 'I do feel sorry for you.'

'It'll never come off,' the Earthworm said brightly. 'Our Centipede will never move again. He will turn into a statue and we shall be able to put him in the middle of the lawn with a bird-bath on the top of his head.'

'We could try peeling him like a banana,' the Old-Green-Grasshopper suggested.

'Or rubbing him with sandpaper,' the Ladybird said.

'Now if he stuck out his tongue,' the Earthworm said, smiling a little for perhaps the first time in his life, 'if he stuck it out really far, then we could all catch hold of it and start pulling. And if we pulled hard enough, we could turn him inside out and he would have a new skin!'

There was a pause while the others considered this interesting proposal.

'I think,' James said slowly, 'I think that the best thing to do . . .' Then he stopped. 'What was *that*?' he asked quickly. 'I heard a voice! I heard someone shouting!'

Thirty

They all raised their heads, listening.

'Ssshh! There it is again!'

But the voice was too far away for them to hear what it was saying.

'It's a Cloud-Man!' Miss Spider cried. 'I just know it's a Cloud-Man! They're after us again!'

'It came from above!' the Earthworm said, and automatically everybody looked upward, everybody except the Centipede, who couldn't move.

'Ouch!' they said. 'Help! Mercy! We're going to catch it this time!' For what they now saw, swirling and twisting directly over their heads, was an immense black cloud, a terrible, dangerous, thundery-looking thing that began to rumble and roar even as they were staring at it. And then, from high up on the top of the cloud, the faraway voice came down to them once again, this time very loud and clear.

'*On with the faucets!*' it shouted. '*On with the faucets! On with the faucets!*'

Three seconds later, the whole underneath of the cloud seemed to split and burst open like a paper bag, and then – *out* came the water! They saw it coming. It was quite easy to see because it wasn't just raindrops. It wasn't raindrops at all. It was a great solid mass of water that might have been a lake or a whole ocean dropping out of the sky on top of them, and down it came, down and down and down, crashing first on to the seagulls and

then on to the peach itself, while the poor travellers shrieked with fear and groped around frantically for something to catch hold of – the peach stem, the silk strings, anything they could find – and all the time the water came pouring and roaring down upon them, bouncing and smashing and sloshing and slashing and swashing and swirling and surging and whirling and gurgling and gushing and rushing and rushing, and it was like being pinncd down underneath the biggest waterfall in the world and not being able to get out. They couldn't speak. They couldn't see. They couldn't breathe. And James Henry Trotter, holding on madly to one of the silk strings above the peach stem, told himself that this must surely be the end of everything at last. But then, just as suddenly as it had started, the deluge stopped. They were out of it and it was all over. The wonderful seagulls had flown right through it and had come out safely on the other side. Once again the giant peach was sailing peacefully through the mysterious moonlit sky.

'I am drowned!' gasped the Old-Green-Grass-hopper, spitting out water by the pint.

'It's gone right through my skin!' the Earthworm groaned. 'I always thought my skin was waterproof but it isn't and now I'm full of rain!'

'*Look at me, look at me!*' shouted the Centipede excitedly. 'It's washed me *clean!* The paint's all gone! I can move again!'

'That's the worst news I've had in a long time,' the Earthworm said.

The Centipede was dancing around the deck and turning somersaults in the air and singing at the top of his voice:

> *'Oh, hooray for the storm and the rain!*
> *I can move! I don't feel any pain!*
> *And now I'm a pest,*
> *I'm the biggest and best,*
> *The most marvellous pest once again!'*

'Oh, do shut up,' the Old-Green-Grasshopper said.
'Look at me!' cried the Centipede.

> *'Look at ME! I am freed! I am freed!*
> *Not a scratch nor a bruise nor a bleed!*
> *To his grave this fine gent*
> *They all thought they had sent*
> *And I very near went!*
> *Oh, I VERY near went!*
> *But they cent quite the wrong Sentipede!'*

Thirty-one

'How fast we are going all of a sudden,' the Ladybird said. 'I wonder why?'

'I don't think the seagulls like this place any

better than we do,' James answered. 'I imagine they want to get out of it as soon as they can. They got a bad fright in that storm we've just been through.'

Faster and faster flew the seagulls, skimming across the sky at a tremendous pace, with the peach trailing out behind them. Cloud after cloud went by on either side, all of them ghostly white in the moonlight, and several more times during the night the travellers caught glimpses of Cloud-Men moving around on the tops of these clouds, working their sinister magic upon the world below.

Once they passed a snow machine in operation, with the Cloud-Men turning the handle and a blizzard of snowflakes blowing out of the great funnel above. They saw the huge drums that were used for making thunder, and the Cloud-Men beating them furiously with long hammers. They saw the frost factories and the wind producers and the places where cyclones and tornadoes were manufactured and sent spinning down towards the Earth, and once, deep in the hollow of a large billowy cloud, they spotted something that could only have been a Cloud-Men's city. There were caves everywhere running into the cloud, and at the entrances to the caves the Cloud-Men's wives were crouching over little stoves with frying-pans in their hands, frying snowballs for their husbands' suppers. And hundreds of Cloud-Men's children were frisking about all over the place and shrieking with laughter and sliding down the billows of the cloud on toboggans.

An hour later, just before dawn, the travellers heard a soft *whooshing* noise above their heads and they glanced up and saw an immense grey batlike creature swooping down towards them out of the dark. It circled round and round the peach, flapping its great wings slowly in the moonlight and staring at the travellers. Then it uttered a series of long deep melancholy cries and flew off again into the night.

'Oh, I do wish the morning would come!' Miss Spider said, shivering all over.

'It won't be long now,' James answered. 'Look, it's getting lighter over there already.'

They all sat in silence watching the sun as it came up slowly over the rim of the horizon for a new day.

Thirty-two

And when full daylight came at last, they all got to their feet and stretched their poor cramped bodies, and then the Centipede, who always seemed to see things first, shouted, 'Look! There's land below!'

'He's right!' they cried, running to the edge of the peach and peering over. 'Hooray! Hooray!'

'It looks like streets and houses!'

'But how enormous it all is!'

A vast city, glistening in the early morning sunshine, lay spread out three thousand feet below them. At that height, the cars were like little beetles crawling along the streets, and people walking on the pavements looked no larger than tiny grains of soot.

'But what tremendous tall buildings!' exclaimed the Ladybird. 'I've never seen anything like *them* before in England. Which town do you think it is?'

'This couldn't possibly be England,' said the Old-Green-Grasshopper.

'Then where is it?' asked Miss Spider.

'You know what those buildings are?' shouted James, jumping up and down with excitement. 'Those are skyscrapers! So this must be America! And that, my friends, means that we have crossed the Atlantic Ocean overnight!'

'You don't mean it!' they cried.

'It's not possible!'

'It's incredible! It's unbelievable!'

'Oh, I've always dreamed of going to America!'

cried the Centipede. 'I had a friend once who – '

'Be quiet!' said the Earthworm. 'Who cares about your friend? The thing we've got to think about now is *how on earth are we going to get down to earth*?'

'Ask James,' said the Ladybird.

'I don't think that should be so very difficult,' James told them. 'All we'll have to do is to cut loose a few seagulls. Not too many, mind you, but just enough so that the others can't *quite* keep us up in the air. Then down we shall go, slowly and gently, until we reach the ground. Centipede will bite through the strings for us one at a time.'

Thirty-three

Far below them, in the City of New York, something like pandemonium was breaking out. A great round ball as big as a house had been sighted hovering high up in the sky over the very centre of Manhattan, and the cry had gone up that it was an enormous bomb sent over by another country to blow the whole city to smithereens. Air-raid sirens began wailing in every section. All radio and television programmes were interrupted with announcements that the population must go down into their cellars immediately. One million people walking in the streets on their way to work looked up into the sky and saw the monster hovering above them, and started running for the nearest

subway entrance to take cover. Generals grabbed hold of telephones and shouted orders to everyone they could think of. The Mayor of New York called up the President of the United States down in Washington, D.C., to ask him for help, and the President, who at that moment was having breakfast in his pyjamas, quickly pushed away his half-finished plate of Sugar Crisps and started pressing buttons right and left to summon his Admirals and his Generals. And all the way across the vast stretch of America, in all the fifty States from Alaska to Florida, from Pennsylvania to Hawaii, the alarm was sounded and the word went out that the biggest bomb in the history of the world was hovering over New York City, and that at any moment it might go off.

Thirty-four

'Come on, Centipede, bite through the first string,' James ordered.

The Centipede took one of the silk strings between his teeth and bit through it. And once again (but *not* with an angry Cloud-Man dangling from the end of the string this time) a single seagull came away from the rest of the flock and went flying off on its own.

'Bite another,' James ordered.

The Centipede bit through another string.

'Why aren't we sinking?'

'We are sinking!'

'No, we're not!'

'Don't forget the peach is a lot lighter now than when we started out,' James told them. 'It lost an awful lot of juice when all those hailstones hit it in the night. Cut away two more seagulls, Centipede!'

'Ah, that's better!'

'Here we go!'

'Now we really are sinking!'

'Yes, this is perfect! Don't bite any more, Centipede, or we'll sink too fast! Gently does it!'

Slowly the great peach began losing height, and the buildings and streets down below began coming closer and closer.

'Do you think we'll all get our pictures in the papers when we get down?' the Ladybird asked.

'My goodness, I've forgotten to polish my boots!' the Centipede said. 'Everyone must help me to polish my boots before we arrive.'

'Oh, for heaven's sake!' said the Earthworm. 'Can't you ever stop thinking about – '

But he never finished his sentence. For suddenly ... *WHOOOSH!* ... and they looked up and saw a huge four-engined plane come shooting out of a near-by cloud and go whizzing past them not more than twenty feet over their heads. This was actually the regular early morning passenger plane coming in to New York from Chicago, and as it went by, it sliced right through every single one of the silken strings, and immediately the seagulls broke away, and the enormous peach, having nothing to hold it up in the air any longer, went tumbling down towards the earth like a lump of lead.

'Help!' cried the Centipede.

'Save us!' cried Miss Spider.

'We are lost!' cried the Ladybird.

'This is the end!' cried the Old-Green-Grasshopper.

'James!' cried the Earthworm. 'Do something, James! Quickly, do something!'

'I can't!' cried James. 'I'm sorry! Good-bye! Shut your eyes everybody! It won't be long now!'

Thirty-five

Round and round and upside down went the peach as it plummeted towards the earth, and they were all clinging desperately to the stem to save themselves from being flung into space.

Faster and faster it fell. Down and down and down, racing closer and closer to the houses and streets below, where it would surely smash into a million pieces when it hit. And all the way along Fifth Avenue and Madison Avenue, and along all the other streets in the City, people who had not yet reached the underground shelters looked up and saw it coming, and they stopped running and stood there staring in a sort of stupor at what they thought was the biggest bomb in all the world falling out of the sky on to their heads. A few women screamed. Others knelt down on the side-walks and began praying aloud. Strong men turned to one another and said things like, 'I guess this is it, Joe,' and 'Good-bye, everybody, good-bye.' And for the next thirty seconds the whole City held its breath, waiting for the end to come.

Thirty-six

'Good-bye, Ladybird!' gasped James, clinging to the stem of the falling peach. 'Good-bye, Centipede. Good-bye, everybody!' There were only a few seconds to go now and it looked as though they were going to fall right in among all the tallest buildings. James could see the skyscrapers rushing up to meet them at the most awful speed, and most of them had square flat tops, but the very tallest of them all had a top that tapered off into a long sharp point – like an enormous silver needle sticking up into the sky.

And it was precisely on to the top of this needle that the peach fell!

There was a squelch. The needle went in deep. And suddenly – there was the giant peach, caught and spiked upon the very pinnacle of the Empire State Building.

Thirty-seven

It was really an amazing sight, and in two or three minutes, as soon as the people below realized that this now couldn't possibly be a bomb, they came pouring out of the shelters and the subways to gape at the marvel. The streets for half a mile around the building were jammed with men and women, and when the word spread that there were actually living things moving about on the top of the great round ball, then everyone went wild with excitement.

'It's a flying saucer!' they shouted.

'They are from Outer Space!'

'They are men from Mars!'

'Or maybe they came from the Moon!'

And a man who had a pair of binoculars to his eyes said, 'They look *pritt*-ty peculiar to me, I'll tell you that.'

Police cars and fire engines came screaming in from all over the city and pulled up outside the Empire State Building. Two hundred firemen and six hundred policemen swarmed into the building and went up in the elevators as high as they could go. Then they poured out on to the observation roof – which is the place where tourists stand – just at the bottom of the big spike.

All the policemen were holding their guns at the ready, with their fingers on the triggers, and the firemen were clutching their hatchets. But from where they stood, almost directly underneath the peach, they couldn't actually see the travellers up on top.

'Ahoy there!' shouted the Chief of Police. 'Come out and show yourselves!'

Suddenly, the great brown head of the Centipede appeared over the side of the peach. His black eyes, as large and round as two marbles, glared down at the policemen and the firemen below. Then his monstrous ugly face broke into a wide grin.

The policemen and the firemen all started shouting at once. 'Look out!' they cried. 'It's a Dragon!'

'It's not a Dragon! It's a Wampus!'

'It's a Gorgon!'

'It's a Sea-serpent!'

'It's a Prock!'

'It's a Manticore!'

Three firemen and five policemen fainted and had to be carried away.

'It's a Snozzwanger!' cried the Chief of Police.

'It's a Whangdoodle!' yelled the Head of the Fire Department.

The Centipede kept on grinning. He seemed to be enjoying enormously the commotion that he was causing.

'Now see here!' shouted the Chief of Police, cupping his hands to his mouth. 'You listen to me! I want you to tell me exactly where you've come from!'

'We've come from thousands of miles away!' the Centipede shouted back, grinning more broadly than ever and showing his brown teeth.

'There you are!' called the Chief of Police. 'I *told* you they came from Mars!'

'I guess you're right!' said the Head of the Fire Department.

At this point, the Old-Green-Grasshopper poked his huge green head over the side of the peach, alongside the Centipede's. Six more big strong men fainted when they saw him.

'That one's an Oinck!' screamed the Head of the Fire Department. 'I just *know* it's an Oinck!'

'Or a Cockatrice!' yelled the Chief of Police. 'Stand back, men! It may jump down on us any moment!'

'What on earth are they talking about?' the Old-Green-Grasshopper said to the Centipede.

'Search me,' the Centipede answered. 'But they seem to be in an awful stew about something.'

Then Miss Spider's large black murderous-looking head, which to a stranger was probably the most terrifying of all, appeared next to the Grasshopper's.

'Snakes and ladders!' yelled the Head of the Fire Department. 'We are finished now! It's a giant Scorpula!'

'It's worse than that!' cried the Chief of Police. 'It's a vermicious Knid! Oh, just look at its vermicious gruesome face!'

'Is that the kind that eats fully-grown men for breakfast?' the Head of the Fire Department asked, going white as a sheet.

'I'm afraid it is,' the Chief of Police answered.

'Oh, *please* why doesn't someone help us to get

down from here?' Miss Spider called out. 'It's making me giddy.'

'This could be a trick!' said the Head of the Fire Department. 'Don't anyone make a move until I say!'

'They've probably got space guns!' muttered the Chief of Police.

'But we've *got* to do *something*!' the Head of the Fire Department announced grimly. 'About five million people are standing down there on the streets watching us.'

331

'Then why don't you put up a ladder?' the Chief of Police asked him. 'I'll stand at the bottom and hold it steady for you while you go up and see what's happening.'

'Thanks very much!' snapped the Head of the Fire Department.

Soon there were no less than *seven* large fantastic faces peering down over the side of the peach – the Centipede's, the Old-Green-Grasshopper's, Miss Spider's, the Earthworm's, the Ladybird's, the Silkworm's, and the Glow-worm's. And a sort of panic was beginning to break out among the firemen and the policemen on the rooftop.

Then, all at once, the panic stopped and a great gasp of astonishment went up all round. For now, a small boy was seen to be standing up there beside the other creatures. His hair was blowing in the wind, and he was laughing and waving and calling out, 'Hello, everybody! Hello!'

For a few moments, the men below just stood and stared and gaped. They simply couldn't believe their eyes.

'*Bless* my soul!' cried the Head of the Fire Department, going red in the face. 'It really *is* a little boy, isn't it?'

'Don't be frightened of us, please!' James called out. 'We are so glad to be here!'

'What about those others beside you?' shouted the Chief of Police. 'Are any of them dangerous?'

'Of course they're not dangerous!' James answered. 'They're the nicest creatures in the world! Allow me to introduce them to you one by one and then I'm sure you will believe me.'

'My friends, this is the Centipede, and let me make it
    known
He is so sweet and gentle that (although he's
    overgrown)
The Queen of Spain, again and again, has summoned
    him by phone
To baby-sit and sing and knit and be a chaperone
When nurse is off and all the royal children are alone.'
('Small wonder,' said a Fireman, 'they're no longer on
    the throne.')

'The Earthworm, on the other hand,'
Said James, beginning to expand,

'Is great for digging up the land
And making old soils newer.
Moreover, you should understand
He would be absolutely grand
For digging subway tunnels and
For making you a sewer.'
(*The Earthworm blushed and beamed with pride.
Miss Spider clapped and cheered and cried,
'Could any words be truer?'*)

'And the Grasshopper, ladies and gents, is a boon
In millions and millions of ways.
You have only to ask him to give you a tune
And he plays and he plays and he plays.
As a toy for your children he's perfectly sweet;
There's nothing so good in the shops –
You've only to tickle the soles of his feet
And he hops and he hops and he hops.'
(*'He can't be very fierce!' exclaimed
The Head of all the Cops.*)

'And now without excuse
I'd like to introduce
This charming Glow-worm, lover of simplicity.
She is easy to install
On your ceiling or your wall,
And although this smacks a bit of eccentricity,
It's really rather clever
For there after you will never
You will NEVER NEVER NEVER
Have the slightest need for using electricity.'
(At which, no less than fifty-two
Policemen cried, 'If this is true
That creature'll get some fabulous publicity!')

'And here we have Miss Spider
With a mile of thread inside her

Who has personally requested me to say
That she's NEVER met Miss Muffet
On her charming little tuffet —
If she had she'd NOT have frightened her away.
Should her looks sometimes alarm you
Then I don't think it would harm you
To repeat at least a hundred times a day:
"I must NEVER kill a spider
I must only help and guide her
And invite her in the nursery to play." '
(The Police all nodded slightly,
And the Firemen smiled politely,
And about a dozen people cried, 'Hooray!')

'And here's my darling Ladybird, so beautjul, so kind,
My greatest comfort since this trip began.
She has four hundred children and she's left them all
    behind,
But they're coming on the next peach of the can.'
(The Cops cried, 'She's entrancing!'
All the Firemen started dancing,
And the crowds all started cheering to a man!)

336

'And now, the Silkworm,' James went on,
'Whose silk will bear comparison
With all the greatest silks there are
In Rome and Philadelphia.
If you would search the whole world through
From Paraguay to Timbuctoo
I don't think you would find one bit
Of silk that could compare with it.
Even the shops in Singapore
Don't have the stuff. And what is more,
This Silkworm had, I'll have you know,
The honour, not so long ago,
To spin and weave and sew and press
The Queen of England's wedding dress.
And she's already made and sent
A waistcoat for your President.'
('Well, good for her!' the Cops cried out,
And all at once a mighty shout
Went up around the Empire State,
Let's get them down at once! Why WAIT?')

337

Thirty-eight

Five minutes later, they were all safely down, and James was excitedly telling his story to a group of flabbergasted officials.

And suddenly – everyone who had come over on the peach was a hero! They were all escorted to the steps of City Hall, where the Mayor of New York made a speech of welcome. And while he was doing this, one hundred steeplejacks, armed with ropes and ladders and pulleys, swarmed up to the top of the Empire State Building and lifted the giant peach off the spike and lowered it to the ground.

Then the Mayor shouted, 'We must now have a ticker-tape parade for our wonderful visitors!'

And so a procession was formed, and in the leading car (which was an enormous open limousine) sat James and all his friends.

Next came the giant peach itself. Men with cranes and hooks had quickly hoisted it on to a very large truck and there it now sat, looking just as huge and proud and brave as ever. There was, of course, a bit of a hole in the bottom of it where the spike of the Empire State Building had gone in, but who cared about that – or indeed about the peach juice that was dripping out of it on to the street?

Behind the peach, skidding about all over the place in the peach juice, came the Mayor's limousine, and behind the Mayor's limousine came about

twenty other limousines carrying all the important people of the City.

And the crowds went wild with excitement. They lined the streets and they leaned out of the windows of the skyscrapers, cheering and yelling and screaming and clapping and throwing out bits of white paper and ticker-tape, and James and his friends stood up in their car and waved back at them as they went by.

Then a rather curious thing happened. The procession was moving slowly along Fifth Avenue when suddenly a little girl in a red dress ran out from the crowd and shouted, 'Oh, James, James! Could I *please* have just a tiny taste of your marvellous peach?'

'Help yourself!' James shouted back. 'Eat all you want! It won't keep for ever, anyway!'

No sooner had he said this than about fifty other children exploded out of the crowd and came running on to the street.

'Can *we* have some, too?' they cried.

'Of course you can!' James answered. 'Everyone can have some!'

The children jumped up on to the truck and swarmed like ants all over the giant peach, eating and eating to their hearts' content. And as the news of what was happening spread quickly from street to street, more and more boys and girls came running from all directions to join the feast. Soon, there was a trail of children a mile long chasing after the peach as it proceeded slowly up Fifth Avenue. Really, it was a fantastic sight. To some

people it looked as though the Pied Piper of Hame-
lin had suddenly descended upon New York. And
to James, who had never dreamed that there could
be so many children as this in the world, it was
the most marvellous thing that had ever
happened.

By the time the procession was over, the whole
gigantic fruit had been completely eaten up, and
only the big brown stone in the middle, licked
clean and shiny by ten thousand eager little
tongues, was left standing on the truck.

Thirty-nine

And thus the journey ended. But the travellers
lived on. Every one of them became rich and
successful in the new country.

The Centipede was made Vice-President-in-
Charge-of-Sales of a high-class firm of boot and
shoe manufacturers.

The Earthworm, with his lovely pink skin, was
employed by a company that made women's face
creams to speak commercials on television.

The Silkworm and Miss Spider, after they had
both been taught to make nylon thread instead of
silk, set up a factory together and made ropes for
tightrope walkers.

The Glow-worm became the light inside the
torch on the Statue of Liberty, and thus saved a

grateful City from having to pay a huge electricity bill every year.

The Old-Green-Grasshopper became a member of the New York Symphony Orchestra, where his playing was greatly admired.

The Ladybird, who had been haunted all her life by the fear that her house was on fire and her children all gone, married the Head of the Fire Department and lived happily ever after.

And as for the enormous peach stone – it was set up permanently in a place of honour in Central Park and became a famous monument. But it was not *only* a famous monument. It was also a famous house. And inside the famous house there lived a famous person –

JAMES HENRY TROTTER

himself.

And all you had to do any day of the week was to go and knock upon the door, and the door would always be opened to you, and you would always be asked to come inside and see the famous room where James had first met his friends. And sometimes, if you were very lucky, you would find the Old-Green-Grasshopper in there as well, resting peacefully in a chair before the fire, or perhaps it would be the Ladybird who had dropped in for a cup of tea and a gossip, or the Centipede to show off a new batch of particularly elegant boots that he had just acquired.

Every day of the week, hundreds and hundreds of children from far and near came pouring into the City to see the marvellous peach stone in the Park. And James Henry Trotter, who once, if you remember, had been the saddest and loneliest little boy that you could find, now had all the friends and playmates in the world. And because so many of them were always begging him to tell and tell again the story of his adventures on the peach, he thought it would be nice if one day he sat down and wrote it as a book.

So he did.

And *that* is what you have just finished reading

Fantastic Mr Fox

To Olivia

Contents

I   The Three Farmers

Down in the valley there were three farms. The owners of
these farms had done well. They were rich men. They
were also nasty men. All three of them were about as nasty
and mean as any men you could meet. Their names were
Farmer Boggis, Farmer Bunce and Farmer Bean.

Boggis was a chicken farmer. He kept thousands of chickens. He was enormously fat. This was because he ate three boiled chickens smothered with dumplings every day for breakfast, lunch and supper.

Bunce was a duck-and-goose farmer. He kept thousands of ducks and geese. He was a kind of pot-bellied dwarf. He was so short his chin would have been underwater in the shallow end of any swimming-pool in the world. His food was doughnuts and goose-livers. He mashed the livers into a disgusting paste and then stuffed the paste into the doughnuts. This diet gave him a tummy-ache and a beastly temper.

Bean was a turkey-and-apple farmer. He kept thousands of turkeys in an orchard full of apple trees. He never ate any food at all. Instead, he drank gallons of strong cider which he made from the apples in his orchard. He was as thin as a pencil and the cleverest of them all.

Boggis and Bunce and Bean
One fat, one short, one lean.
These horrible crooks
So different in looks
Were none the less equally mean.

That is what the children round about used to sing when they saw them.

2   Mr Fox

On a hill above the valley there was a wood.

In the wood there was a huge tree.

Under the tree there was a hole.

In the hole lived Mr Fox and Mrs Fox and their four Small Foxes.

Every evening as soon as it got dark, Mr Fox would say to Mrs Fox, 'Well, my darling, what shall it be this time? A plump chicken from Boggis? A duck or a goose from Bunce? Or a nice turkey from Bean?' And when Mrs Fox had told him what she wanted, Mr Fox would creep down into the valley in the darkness of the night and help himself.

Boggis and Bunce and Bean knew very well what was going on, and it made them wild with rage. They were not men who liked to give anything away. Less still did they like anything to be stolen from them. So every night each of them would take his shotgun and hide in a dark place somewhere on his own farm, hoping to catch the robber.

But Mr Fox was too clever for them. He always approached a farm with the wind blowing in his face, and this meant that if any man were lurking in the shadows ahead, the wind would carry the smell of that man to Mr Fox's nose from far away. Thus, if Mr Boggis was hiding behind his Chicken House Number One, Mr Fox would smell him out from fifty yards off and quickly change direction, heading for Chicken House Number Four at the other end of the farm.

'Dang and blast that lousy beast!' cried Boggis.

'I'd like to rip his guts out!' said Bunce.

'He must be killed!' cried Bean.

'But how?' said Boggis. 'How on earth can we catch the blighter?'

Bean picked his nose delicately with a long finger. 'I have a plan,' he said.

'You've never had a decent plan yet,' said Bunce.

'Shut up and listen,' said Bean. 'Tomorrow night we will all hide just outside the hole where the fox lives. We will wait there until he comes out. Then ... *Bang! Bang-bang-bang.*'

'Very clever,' said Bunce. 'But first we shall have to find the hole.'

'My dear Bunce, I've already found it,' said the crafty Bean. 'It's up in the wood on the hill. It's under a huge tree ...'

3   The Shooting

'Well, my darling,' said Mr Fox. 'What shall it be tonight?'

'I think we'll have duck tonight,' said Mrs Fox.

'Bring us two fat ducks, if you please. One for you and me, and one for the children.'

'Ducks it shall be!' said Mr Fox. 'Bunce's best!'

'Now do be careful,' said Mrs Fox.

'My darling,' said Mr Fox, 'I can smell those goons a mile away. I can even smell one from the other. Boggis gives off a filthy stink of rotten chicken-skins. Bunce reeks of goose-livers, and as for Bean, the fumes of apple cider hang around him like poisonous gases.'

'Yes, but just don't get careless,' said Mrs Fox. 'You know they'll be waiting for you, all three of them.'

'Don't you worry about me,' said Mr Fox. 'I'll see you later.'

But Mr Fox would not have been quite so cocky had he known exactly *where* the three farmers were waiting at that moment. They were just outside the entrance to the hole, each one crouching behind a tree with his gun loaded. And what is more, they had chosen their positions very carefully, making sure that the wind was not blowing from them towards the fox's hole. In fact, it was blowing in the opposite direction. There was no chance of them being 'smelled out'.

Mr Fox crept up the dark tunnel to the mouth of his hole. He poked his long handsome face out into the night air and sniffed once.

He moved an inch or two forward and stopped.

He sniffed again. He was always especially careful when coming out from his hole.

He inched forward a little more. The front half of his body was now in the open.

His black nose twitched from side to side, sniffing and sniffing for the scent of danger. He found none, and he was just about to go trotting forward into the wood when he heard or thought he heard a tiny noise, a soft rustling sound, as though someone had moved a foot ever so gently through a patch of dry leaves.

Mr Fox flattened his body against the ground and lay very still, his ears pricked. He waited a long time, but he heard nothing more.

'It must have been a field-mouse,' he told himself, 'or some other small animal.'

He crept a little further out of the hole . . . then further still. He was almost right out in the open now. He took a last careful look around. The wood was murky and very still. Somewhere in the sky the moon was shining.

Just then, his sharp night-eyes caught a glint of something bright behind a tree not far away. It was a small silver speck of moonlight shining on a polished surface. Mr Fox lay still, watching it. What on earth was it? Now it was moving. It was coming up and up . . . *Great heavens! It was the barrel of a gun!* Quick as a whip, Mr Fox jumped back into his hole and at that same instant the entire wood seemed to explode around him. *Bang-bang! Bang-bang! Bang-bang!*

The smoke from the three guns floated upward in the night air. Boggis and Bunce and Bean came out from behind their trees and walked towards the hole.

'Did we get him?' said Bean.

One of them shone a flashlight on the hole, and there on

the ground, in the circle of light, half in and half out of the
hole, lay the poor tattered bloodstained remains of . . . a
fox's tail. Bean picked it up. 'We got the tail but we
missed the fox,' he said, tossing the thing away.

'Dang and blast!' said Boggis. 'We shot too late. We
should have let fly the moment he poked his head out.'

'He won't be poking it out again in a hurry,' Bunce
said.

Bean pulled a flask from his pocket and took a swig of cider. Then he said, 'It'll take three days at least before he gets hungry enough to come out again. I'm not sitting around here waiting for that. Let's dig him out.'

'Ah,' said Boggis. 'Now you're talking sense. We can dig him out in a couple of hours. We know he's there.'

'I reckon there's a whole family of them down that hole,' Bunce said.

'Then we'll have the lot,' said Bean. 'Get the shovels!'

4 The Terrible Shovels

Down the hole, Mrs Fox was tenderly licking the stump of Mr Fox's tail to stop the bleeding. 'It was the finest tail for miles around,' she said between licks.

'It hurts,' said Mr Fox.

'I know it does, sweetheart. But it'll soon get better.'

'And it will soon grow again, Dad,' said one of the Small Foxes.

'It will never grow again,' said Mr Fox. 'I shall be tail-less for the rest of my life.' He looked very glum.

There was no food for the foxes that night, and soon the children dozed off. Then Mrs Fox dozed off. But Mr Fox couldn't sleep because of the pain in the stump of his tail. 'Well,' he thought, 'I suppose I'm lucky to be alive at all. And now they've found our hole, we're going to have to move out as soon as possible. We'll never get any peace if we . . . What was *that*?' He turned his head sharply and listened. The noise he heard now was the most frightening noise a fox can ever hear – the scrape-scrape-scraping of shovels digging into the soil.

'Wake up!' he shouted. 'They're digging us out!'

Mrs Fox was wide awake in one second. She sat up, quivering all over. 'Are you sure that's it?' she whispered.

'I'm positive! Listen!'

'They'll kill my children!' cried Mrs Fox.

'Never!' said Mr Fox.

'But darling, they will!' sobbed Mrs Fox. 'You know they will!'

Scrunch, scrunch, scrunch went the shovels above their heads. Small stones and bits of earth began falling from the roof of the tunnel.

'How will they kill us, Mummy?' asked one of the Small Foxes. His round black eyes were huge with fright. 'Will there be dogs?' he said.

Mrs Fox began to cry. She gathered her four children close to her and held them tight.

Suddenly there was an especially loud crunch above their heads and the sharp end of a shovel came right through the ceiling. The sight of this awful thing seemed to have an electric effect upon Mr Fox. He jumped up and shouted, 'I've got it! Come on! There's not a moment to lose! Why didn't I think of it before!'

'Think of what, Dad?'

'A fox can dig quicker than a man!' shouted Mr Fox, beginning to dig. 'Nobody in the world can dig as quick as a fox!'

The soil began to fly out furiously behind Mr Fox as he started to dig for dear life with his front feet. Mrs Fox ran forward to help him. So did the four children.

'Go downwards!' ordered Mr Fox. 'We've got to go deep! As deep as we possibly can!'

The tunnel began to grow longer and longer. It sloped steeply downward. Deeper and deeper below the surface of the ground it went. The mother and the father and all four of the children were digging together. Their front legs were moving so fast you couldn't see them. And gradually the scrunching and scraping of the shovels became fainter and fainter.

After about an hour, Mr Fox stopped digging. 'Hold it!' he said. They all stopped. They turned and looked back up the long tunnel they had just dug. All was quiet. 'Phew!' said Mr Fox. 'I think we've done it! They'll never get as deep as this. Well done, everyone!'

They all sat down, panting for breath. And Mrs Fox said to her children, 'I should like you to know that if it wasn't for your father we should all be dead by now. Your father is a fantastic fox.'

Mr Fox looked at his wife and she smiled. He loved her more than ever when she said things like that.

5   The Terrible Tractors

As the sun rose the next morning, Boggis and Bunce and Bean were still digging. They had dug a hole so deep you could have put a house into it. But they had not yet come to the end of the foxes' tunnel. They were all very tired and cross.

'Dang and blast!' said Boggis. 'Whose rotten idea was this?'

'Bean's idea,' said Bunce.

Boggis and Bunce both stared at Bean. Bean took another swig of cider, then put the flask back into his pocket without offering it to the others. 'Listen,' he said angrily, 'I want that fox! I'm going to get that fox! I'm not giving in till I've strung him up over my front porch, dead as a dumpling!'

'We can't get him by digging, that's for sure,' said the fat Boggis. 'I've had enough of digging.'

Bunce, the little pot-bellied dwarf, looked up at Bean and said, 'Have you got any more stupid ideas, then?'

'What?' said Bean. 'I can't hear you.' Bean never took a bath. He never even washed. As a result, his earholes were clogged with all kinds of muck and wax and bits of chewing-gum and dead flies and stuff like that. This made him deaf. 'Speak louder,' he said to Bunce, and Bunce shouted back, 'Got any more stupid ideas?'

Bean rubbed the back of his neck with a dirty finger. He had a boil coming there and it itched. 'What we need on this job,' he said, 'is machines . . . *mechanical* shovels. We'll have him out in five minutes with *mechanical* shovels.'

This was a pretty good idea and the other two had to admit it.

'All right then,' Bean said, taking charge. 'Boggis, you stay here and see the fox doesn't escape. Bunce and I will go and fetch our machinery. If he tries to get out, shoot him quick.'

The long, thin Bean walked away. The tiny Bunce trotted after him. The fat Boggis stayed where he was with his gun pointing at the fox-hole.

Soon, two enormous caterpillar tractors with mechanical shovels on their front ends came clanking into the wood.

Bean was driving one. Bunce the other. The machines were both black. They were murderous, brutal-looking monsters.

'Here we go, then!' shouted Bean.

'Death to the fox!' shouted Bunce.

The machines went to work, biting huge mouthfuls of soil out of the hill. The big tree under which Mr Fox had dug his hole in the first place was toppled like a matchstick. On all sides, rocks were sent flying and trees were falling and the noise was deafening.

Down in the tunnel the foxes crouched, listening to the terrible clanging and banging overhead. 'What's happening, Dad?' cried the Small Foxes. 'What are they doing?'

Mr Fox didn't know what was happening or what they were doing.

'It's an earthquake!' cried Mrs Fox.

'Look!' said one of the Small Foxes. 'Our tunnel's got shorter! I can see daylight!'

They all looked round, and yes, the mouth of the tunnel was only a few feet away from them now, and in the circle of daylight beyond they could see the two huge black tractors almost on top of them.

'Tractors!' shouted Mr Fox. 'And *mechanical* shovels! Dig for your lives! *Dig, dig, dig!*'

6   The Race

Now there began a desperate race, the machines against the foxes. In the beginning, the hill looked like this:

After about an hour, as the machines bit away more and more soil from the hilltop, it looked like this:

Sometimes the foxes would gain a little ground and the clanking noises would grow fainter and Mr Fox would say, 'We're going to make it! I'm sure we are!' But then a few moments later, the machines would come back at them and the crunch of the mighty shovels would get louder and louder. Once the foxes actually saw the sharp metal edge of one of the shovels as it scraped up the earth just behind them.

'Keep going, my darlings!' panted Mr Fox. 'Don't give up!'

'Keep going!' the fat Boggis shouted to Bunce and Bean. 'We'll get him any moment now!'

'Have you caught sight of him yet?' Bean called back.

'Not yet,' shouted Boggis. 'But I think you're close!'

'I'll pick him up with my bucket!' shouted Bunce. 'I'll chop him to pieces!'

But by lunchtime the machines were still at it. And so were the poor foxes. The hill now looked like this:

The farmers didn't stop for lunch; they were too keen to finish the job.

'Hey there, Mr Fox!' yelled Bunce, leaning out of his tractor. 'We're coming to get you now!'

'You've had your last chicken!' yelled Boggis. 'You'll never come prowling around *my* farm again!'

A sort of madness had taken hold of the three men. The tall skinny Bean and dwarfish pot-bellied Bunce were driving their machines like maniacs, racing the motors and making the shovels dig at a terrific speed. The fat Boggis was hopping about like a dervish and shouting, 'Faster! Faster!'

By five o'clock in the afternoon this is what had happened to the hill:

The hole the machines had dug was like the crater of a volcano. It was such an extraordinary sight that crowds of people came rushing out from the surrounding villages to have a look. They stood on the edge of the crater and stared down at Boggis and Bunce and Bean.

'Hey there, Boggis! What's going on?'

'We're after a fox!'

'You must be mad!'

The people jeered and laughed. But this only made the three farmers more furious and more obstinate and more determined than ever not to give up until they had caught the fox.

7 'We'll Never Let Him Go'

At six o'clock in the evening, Bean switched off the motor of his tractor and climbed down from the driver's seat. Bunce did the same. Both men had had enough. They were tired and stiff from driving the tractors all day. They were also hungry. Slowly they walked over to the small fox's hole in the bottom of the huge crater. Bean's face was purple with rage. Bunce was cursing the fox with dirty words that cannot be printed. Boggis came waddling up. 'Dang and blast that filthy stinking fox!' he said. 'What the heck do we do now?'

'I'll tell you what we *don't* do,' Bean said. 'We don't let him go!'

'We'll never let him go!' Bunce declared.

'Never never never!' cried Boggis.

'Did you hear that, Mr Fox!' yelled Bean, bending low and shouting down the hole. 'It's not over yet, Mr Fox! We're not going home till we've strung you up dead as a dingbat!' Whereupon the three men all shook hands with one another and swore a solemn oath that they would not go back to their farms until the fox was caught.

'What's the next move?' asked Bunce, the pot-bellied dwarf.

'We're sending you down the hole to fetch him up,' said Bean. 'Down you go, you miserable midget!'

'Not me!' screamed Bunce, running away.

Bean made a sickly smile. When he smiled you saw his scarlet gums. You saw more gums than teeth. 'Then there's only one thing to do,' he said. 'We starve him out. We camp here day and night watching the hole. He'll come out in the end. He'll have to.'

So Boggis and Bunce and Bean sent messages down to their farms asking for tents, sleeping-bags and supper.

8   The Foxes Begin to Starve

That evening three tents were put up in the crater on the hill – one for Boggis, one for Bunce and one for Bean. The tents surrounded Mr Fox's hole. And the three farmers sat outside their tents eating their supper. Boggis had three boiled chickens smothered in dumplings, Bunce had six doughnuts filled with disgusting goose-liver paste, and Bean had two gallons of cider. All three of them kept their guns beside them.

Boggis picked up a steaming chicken and held it close to the fox's hole. 'Can you smell this, Mr Fox?' he shouted. 'Lovely tender chicken! Why don't you come up and get it?'

The rich scent of chicken wafted down the tunnel to where the foxes were crouching.

'Oh, Dad,' said one of the Small Foxes, 'couldn't we just sneak up and snatch it out of his hand?'

'Don't you dare!' said Mrs Fox. 'That's just what they want you to do.'

'But we're so *hungry!*' they cried. 'How long will it be till we get something to eat?'

Their mother didn't answer them. Nor did their father. There was no answer to give.

As darkness fell, Bunce and Bean switched on the power-ful headlamps of the two tractors and shone them on to the hole. 'Now,' said Bean, 'we'll take it in turn to keep watch. One watches while two sleep, and so on all through the night.'

Boggis said, 'What if the fox digs a hole right through the hill and comes out on the other side? You didn't think of that one, did you?'

'Of course I did,' said Bean, pretending he had.

'Go on, then, tell us the answer,' said Boggis.

Bean picked something small and black out of his ear and flicked it away. 'How many men have you got working on your farm?' he asked.

'Thirty-five,' Boggis said.

'I've got thirty-six,' Bunce said.

'And I've got thirty-seven,' Bean said. 'That makes one hundred and eight men altogether. We must order them to surround the hill. Each man will have a gun and a flashlight. There will be no escape then for Mr Fox.'

So the order went down to the farms, and that night one hundred and eight men formed a tight ring around the bottom of the hill. They were armed with sticks and guns and hatchets and pistols and all sorts of other horrible weapons. This made it quite impossible for a fox or indeed for any other animal to escape from the hill.

The next day, the watching and waiting went on. Boggis and Bunce and Bean sat upon small stools, staring at the fox's hole. They didn't talk much. They just sat there with their guns on their laps.

Every so often, Mr Fox would creep a little closer towards the mouth of the tunnel and take a sniff. Then he would creep back again and say, 'They're still there.'

'Are you quite sure?' Mrs Fox would ask.

'Positive,' said Mr Fox. 'I can smell that man Bean a mile away. He stinks.'

9   Mr Fox Has a Plan

For three days and three nights this waiting–game went on.

'How long can a fox go without food or water?' Boggis asked on the third day.

'Not much longer now,' Bean told him. 'He'll make a run for it soon. He'll have to.'

Bean was right. Down in the tunnel the foxes were slowly but surely starving to death.

'If only we could have just a tiny sip of water,' said one of the Small Foxes. 'Oh, Dad, can't you do *something*?'

'Couldn't we make a dash for it, Dad? We'd have a little bit of a chance, wouldn't we?'

'No chance at all,' snapped Mrs Fox. 'I refuse to let you go up there and face those guns. I'd sooner you stay down here and die in peace.'

Mr Fox had not spoken for a long time. He had been sitting quite still, his eyes closed, not even hearing what the others were saying. Mrs Fox knew that he was trying desperately to think of a way out. And now, as she looked at him, she saw him stir himself and get slowly to his feet. He looked back at his wife. There was a little spark of excitement dancing in his eyes.

'What is it, darling?' said Mrs Fox quickly.

'I've just had a bit of an idea,' Mr Fox said carefully.

'What?' they cried. 'Oh, Dad, what is it?'

'Come *on!*' said Mrs Fox. 'Tell us quickly!'

'Well . . .' said Mr Fox, then he stopped and sighed and sadly shook his head. He sat down again. 'It's no good,' he said. 'It won't work after all.'

'Why not, Dad?'

'Because it means more digging and we aren't any of us

strong enough for that after three days and nights without food.'

'Yes we are, Dad!' cried the Small Foxes, jumping up and running to their father. 'We can do it! You see if we can't! So can you!'

Mr Fox looked at the four Small Foxes and he smiled. What fine children I have, he thought. They are starving to death and they haven't had a drink for three days, but they are still undefeated. I must not let them down.

'I . . . I suppose we could give it a try,' he said.

'Let's go, Dad! Tell us what you want us to do!'

Slowly, Mrs Fox got to her feet. She was suffering more than any of them from the lack of food and water. She was very weak. 'I am so sorry,' she said, 'but I don't think I am going to be much help.'

'You stay right where you are, my darling,' said Mr Fox. 'We can handle this by ourselves.'

10 Boggis's Chicken House Number One

'This time we must go in a very special direction,' said Mr Fox, pointing sideways and downward.

So he and his four children started to dig once again. The work went much more slowly now. Yet they kept at it with great courage, and little by little the tunnel began to grow.

'Dad, I wish you would tell us *where* we are going,' said one of the children.

'I dare not do that,' said Mr Fox, 'because this place I am *hoping* to get to is so *marvellous* that if I described it to you now you would go crazy with excitement. And then, if we failed to get there (which is very possible), you would die of disappointment. I don't want to raise your hopes too much, my darlings.'

For a long long time they kept on digging. For how long they did not know, because there were no days and no nights down there in the murky tunnel. But at last Mr Fox gave the order to stop. 'I think,' he said, 'we had better take a peep upstairs now and see where we are. I know where I *want* to be, but I can't possibly be sure we're anywhere near it.'

Slowly, wearily, the foxes began to slope the tunnel up towards the surface. Up and up it went . . . until suddenly they came to something hard above their heads and they couldn't go up any further. Mr Fox reached up to examine this hard thing. 'It's wood!' he whispered. 'Wooden planks!'

'What does that mean, Dad?'

'It means, unless I am very much mistaken, that we are right underneath somebody's house,' whispered Mr Fox. 'Be very quiet now while I take a peek.'

Carefully, Mr Fox began pushing up one of the floorboards. The board creaked most terribly and they all ducked down, waiting for something awful to happen. Nothing did. So Mr Fox pushed up a second board. And then, very very cautiously, he poked his head up through the gap. He let out a shriek of excitement.

'*I've done it!*' he yelled. '*I've done it first time! I've done it! I've done it!*' He pulled himself up through the gap in the floor and started prancing and dancing with joy. 'Come on up!' he sang out. 'Come up and see where you are, my darlings! What a sight for a hungry fox! Hallelujah! Hooray! Hooray!'

The four Small Foxes scrambled up out of the tunnel and what a fantastic sight it was that now met their eyes! They were in a huge shed and the whole place was teeming with chickens. There were white chickens and brown chickens and black chickens by the thousand!

'Boggis's Chicken House Number One!' cried Mr Fox. 'It's exactly what I was aiming at! I hit it slap in the middle! First time! Isn't that fantastic! *And*, if I may say so, rather clever!'

The Small Foxes went wild with excitement. They started running around in all directions, chasing the stupid chickens.

'Wait!' ordered Mr Fox. 'Don't lose your heads! Stand back! Calm down! Let's do this properly! First of all, everyone have a drink of water!'

They all ran over to the chickens' drinking-trough and lapped up the lovely cool water. Then Mr Fox chose three of the plumpest hens, and with a clever flick of his jaws he killed them instantly.

'Back to the tunnel!' he ordered. 'Come on! No fooling around! The quicker you move, the quicker you shall have something to eat!'

One after another, they climbed down through the hole in the floor and soon they were all standing once again in the dark tunnel. Mr Fox reached up and pulled the floorboards back into place. He did this with great care. He did it so that no one could tell they had ever been moved.

'My son,' he said, giving the three plump hens to the biggest of his four small children, 'run back with these to your mother. Tell her to prepare a feast. Tell her the rest of us will be along in a jiffy, as soon as we have made a few other little arrangements.'

11　A Surprise for Mrs Fox

The Small Fox ran back along the tunnel as fast as he could, carrying the three plump hens. He was exploding with joy. 'Just wait!' he kept thinking, 'just wait till Mummy sees these!' He had a long way to run but he never stopped once on the way and he came bursting in upon Mrs Fox. 'Mummy!' he cried, out of breath. 'Look, Mummy, look! Wake up and see what I've brought you!'

Mrs Fox, who was weaker than ever now from lack of food, opened one eye and looked at the hens. 'I'm dreaming,' she murmured and closed the eye again.

'You're not dreaming, Mummy! They're real chickens! We're saved! We're not going to starve!'

Mrs Fox opened both eyes and sat up quickly. 'But, my *dear* child!' she cried. 'Where on earth . . .?'

'Boggis's Chicken House Number One!' spluttered the Small Fox. 'We tunnelled right up under the floor and you've never seen so many big fat hens in all your life! And Dad said to prepare a feast! They'll be back soon!'

The sight of food seemed to give new strength to Mrs Fox. 'A feast it shall be!' she said, standing up. 'Oh, what a fantastic fox your father is! Hurry up, child, and start plucking those chickens!'

Far away down in the tunnel, the fantastic Mr Fox was saying, 'Now for the next bit, my darlings! This one'll be as easy as pie! All we have to do is dig another little tunnel from *here* to there!'

'To where, Dad?'

'Don't ask so many questions. Start digging!'

12   Badger

Mr Fox and the three remaining Small Foxes dug fast and straight. They were all too excited now to feel tired or hungry. They knew they were going to have a whacking great feast before long and the fact that it was none other than Boggis's chickens they were going to eat made them churgle with laughter every time they thought of it. It was lovely to realize that while the fat farmer was sitting up there on the hill waiting for them to starve, he was also giving them their dinner without knowing it. 'Keep digging,' said Mr Fox. 'It's not much further.'

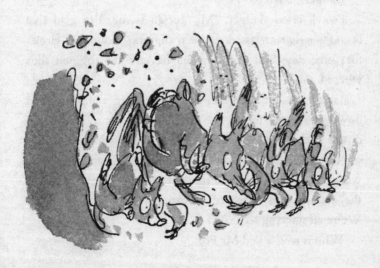

All of a sudden a deep voice above their heads said, *'Who goes there?'* The foxes jumped. They looked up quickly and they saw, peeking through a small hole in the roof of the tunnel, a long black pointed furry face.

'Badger!' cried Mr Fox.

'Foxy!' cried Badger. 'My goodness me, I'm glad I've found *someone* at last! I've been digging around in circles for three days and nights and I haven't the foggiest idea where I am!'

Badger made the hole in the ceiling bigger and dropped down beside the foxes. A Small Badger (his son) dropped down after him. 'Haven't you *heard* what's happening up on the hill?' Badger said excitedly. 'It's chaos! Half the wood has disappeared and there are men with guns all over the countryside! None of us can get out, even at night! We're all starving to death!'

'Who is *we*?' asked Mr Fox.

'All us diggers. That's me and Mole and Rabbit and all our wives and children. Even Weasel, who can usually sneak out of the tightest spots, is right now hiding down my hole with Mrs Weasel and six kids. What on earth are we going to do, Foxy? I think we're finished!'

Mr Fox looked at his three children and he smiled. The children smiled back at him, sharing his secret. 'My dear old Badger,' he said, 'this mess you're in is all my fault . . .'

'I *know* it's your fault!' said Badger furiously. 'And the farmers are not going to give up till they've got you. Unfortunately, that means *us* as well. It means everyone on the hill.' Badger sat down and put a paw around his small son. 'We're done for,' he said softly. 'My poor wife up there is so weak she can't dig another yard.'

'Nor can mine,' said Mr Fox. 'And yet at this very minute she is preparing for me and my children the most delicious feast of plump juicy chickens . . .'

'Stop!' cried Badger. 'Don't tease me! I can't stand it!'

'It's true!' cried the Small Foxes. 'Dad's not teasing! We've got chickens galore!'

'And because everything is entirely my fault,' said Mr Fox, 'I invite you to share the feast. I invite *everyone* to share it – you and Mole and Rabbit and Weasel and all your wives and children. There'll be plenty to go round, I can assure you.'

'You mean it?' cried Badger. 'You *really mean* it?'

Mr Fox pushed his face close to Badger's and whispered darkly, '*Do you know* where we've just been?'

'Where?'

'Right inside Boggis's Chicken House Number One!'

'No!'

'Yes! But that is nothing to where we are going now. You have come just at the right moment, my dear Badger. You can help us dig. And in the meanwhile, your small son can run back to Mrs Badger and all the others and spread the good news.' Mr Fox turned to the Small Badger and said, 'Tell them they are invited to a Fox's Feast. Then bring them all down here and follow this tunnel back until you find my home!'

'Yes, Mr Fox!' said the Small Badger. 'Yes, sir! Right away, sir! Oh, thank you, sir!' and he scrambled quickly back through the hole in the roof of the tunnel and disappeared.

13   Bunce's Giant Storehouse

'My dear Foxy!' cried Badger. 'What in the world has happened to your tail?'

'Don't talk about it, *please*,' said Mr Fox. 'It's a painful subject.'

They were digging the new tunnel. They dug on in silence. Badger was a great digger and the tunnel went forward at a terrific pace now that he was lending a paw. Soon they were crouching underneath yet another wooden floor.

Mr Fox grinned slyly, showing sharp white teeth. 'If I am not mistaken, my dear Badger,' he said, 'we are now underneath the farm which belongs to that nasty little pot-

bellied dwarf, Bunce. We are, in fact, directly underneath the most *interesting part* of that farm.'

'Ducks and geese!' cried the Small Foxes, licking their lips. 'Juicy tender ducks and big fat geese!'

'Ex-*actly!*' said Mr Fox.

'But how in the world can you know where we are?' asked Badger.

Mr Fox grinned again, showing even more white teeth. 'Look,' he said, 'I know my way around these farms blindfold. For me it's just as easy below ground as it is above it.' He reached high and pushed up one wooden floorboard, then another. He poked his head through the gap.

'Yes!' he shouted, jumping up into the room above. 'I've done it again! I've hit it smack on the nose! Right in the bull's-eye! Come and look!'

Quickly Badger and the three Small Foxes scrambled up after him. They stopped and stared. They stood and gaped. They were so overwhelmed they couldn't speak; for what they now saw was a kind of fox's dream, a badger's dream, a paradise for hungry animals.

'This, my dear old Badger,' proclaimed Mr Fox, 'is Bunce's Mighty Storehouse! All his finest stuff is stored in here before he sends it off to market.'

Against all the four walls of the great room, stacked in cupboards and piled upon shelves reaching from floor to ceiling, were thousands and thousands of the finest and fattest ducks and geese, plucked and ready for roasting! And up above, dangling from the rafters, there must have been at least a hundred smoked hams and fifty sides of bacon!

'Just feast your eyes on *that!*' cried Mr Fox, dancing up and down. 'What d'you think of it, eh? Pretty good grub!'

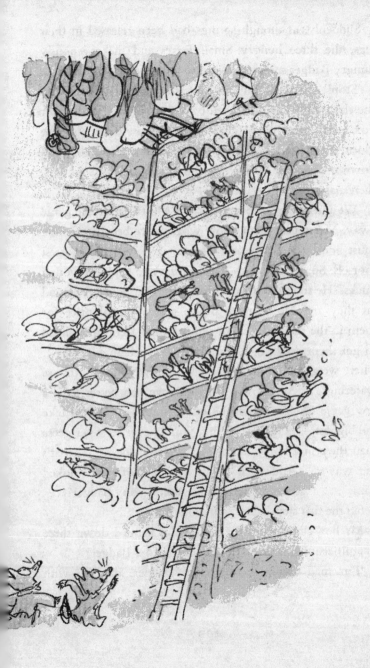

Suddenly, as though springs had been released in their legs, the three hungry Small Foxes and the ravenously hungry Badger sprang forward to grab the luscious food.

'Stop!' ordered Mr Fox. 'This is *my* party, so *I* shall do the choosing.' The others fell back, licking their chops. Mr Fox began prowling around the storehouse examining the glorious display with an expert eye. A thread of saliva slid down one side of his jaw and hung suspended in mid-air, then snapped.

'We mustn't overdo it,' he said. 'Mustn't give the game away. Mustn't let them know what we've been up to. We must be neat and tidy and take just a few of the choicest morsels. So, to start with we shall have four plump young ducks.' He took them from the shelf. 'Oh, how lovely and fat they are! No wonder Bunce gets a special price for them in the market! . . . All right, Badger, lend me a hand to get them down . . . You children can help as well . . . There we go . . . Goodness me, look how your mouths are watering . . . And now . . . I think we had better have a few geese . . . Three will be quite enough . . . We'll take the biggest . . . Oh my, oh my, you'll never see finer geese than these in a king's kitchen . . . Gently does it . . . that's the way . . . And what about a couple of nice smoked hams . . . I adore smoked ham, don't you, Badger? . . . Fetch me that step-ladder, will you please . . .'

Mr Fox climbed up the ladder and handed down three magnificent hams. 'And do you like bacon, Badger?'

'I'm mad about bacon!' cried Badger, dancing with

excitement. 'Let's have a side of bacon! That big one up there!'

'And carrots, Dad!' said the smallest of the three Small Foxes. 'We must take some of those carrots.'

'Don't be a twerp,' said Mr Fox. 'You know we never eat things like that.'

'It's not for us, Dad. It's for the Rabbits. They only eat vegetables.'

'My goodness me, you're right!' cried Mr Fox. 'What a thoughtful little fellow you are! Take ten bunches of carrots!'

Soon, all this lovely loot was lying in a neat heap upon the floor. The Small Foxes crouched close, their noses twitching, their eyes shining like stars.

'And now,' said Mr Fox, 'we shall have to borrow from our friend Bunce two of those useful push-carts over in the corner.' He and Badger fetched the push-carts, and the ducks and geese and hams and bacon were loaded on to them. Quickly the push-carts were lowered through the hole in the floor. The animals slid down after them. Back in the tunnel, Mr Fox again pulled the floorboards very carefully into place so that no one could see they had been moved.

'My darlings,' he said, pointing to two of the three Small Foxes, 'take a cart each and run back as fast as you can to your mother. Give her my love and tell her we are having guests for dinner – the Badgers, the Moles, the Rabbits and the Weasels. Tell her it must be a truly great feast. And tell her the rest of us will be home as soon as we've done one more little job.'

'Yes, Dad! Right away, Dad!' they answered, and they grabbed a trolley each and went rushing off down the tunnel.

14   Badger Has Doubts

'Just one more visit!' cried Mr Fox.

'And I'll bet I know where that'll be,' said the only Small Fox now left. He was the Smallest Fox of them all.

'Where?' asked Badger.

'Well,' said the Smallest Fox. 'We've been to Boggis and we've been to Bunce but we haven't been to Bean. It must be Bean.'

'You are right,' said Mr Fox. 'But what you don't know is which *part* of Bean's place we are about to visit.'

'Which?' they said both together.

'Ah-ha,' said Mr Fox. 'Just you wait and see.' They were digging as they talked. The tunnel was going forward fast.

Suddenly Badger said, 'Doesn't this worry you just a tiny bit, Foxy?'

'Worry me?' said Mr Fox. 'What?'

'All this . . . this *stealing*.'

Mr Fox stopped digging and stared at Badger as though he had gone completely dotty. 'My dear old furry frump,' he said, 'do you know anyone in the *whole world* who wouldn't swipe a few chickens if his children were starving to death?'

There was a short silence while Badger thought deeply about this.

'You are far too respectable,' said Mr Fox.

'There's nothing wrong with being respectable,' Badger said.

'Look,' said Mr Fox, 'Boggis and Bunce and Bean are out to *kill* us. You realize that, I hope?'

'I do, Foxy, I do indeed,' said the gentle Badger.

'But *we're* not going to stoop to *their* level. We don't want to kill *them*.'

'I should hope not, indeed,' said Badger.

'We wouldn't dream of it,' said Mr Fox. 'We shall simply take a little food here and there to keep us and our families alive. Right?'

'I suppose we'll have to,' said Badger.

'If *they* want to be horrible, let them,' said Mr Fox. 'We down here are decent peace-loving people.'

Badger laid his head on one side and smiled at Mr Fox. 'Foxy,' he said, 'I love you.'

'Thank you,' said Mr Fox. 'And now let's get on with the digging.'

Five minutes later, Badger's front paws hit against something flat and hard. 'What on earth is this?' he said. 'It looks like a solid stone wall.' He and Mr Fox scraped away the soil. It *was* a wall. But it was built of bricks, not stones. The wall was right in front of them, blocking their way.

'Now who in the world would build a wall under the ground?' asked Badger.

'Very simple,' said Mr Fox. 'It's the wall of an underground room. And if I am not mistaken, it is exactly what I'm looking for.'

15 Bean's Secret Cider Cellar

Mr Fox examined the wall carefully. He saw that the cement between the bricks was old and crumbly, so he loosened a brick without much trouble and pulled it away. Suddenly, out from the hole where the brick had been, there popped a small sharp face with whiskers, 'Go away!' it snapped. 'You can't come in here! It's private!'

'Good Lord!' said Badger. 'It's Rat!'

'You saucy beast!' said Mr Fox. 'I should have guessed we'd find you down here somewhere.'

'Go away!' shrieked Rat. 'Go on, beat it! This is my private pitch!'

'Shut up,' said Mr Fox.

'I will not shut up!' shrieked Rat. 'This is *my* place! I got here first!'

Mr Fox gave a brilliant smile, flashing his white teeth. 'My dear Rat,' he said softly, 'I am a hungry fellow and if you don't hop it quickly I shall eat-you-up-in-one-gulp!'

That did it. Rat popped back fast out of sight. Mr Fox laughed and began pulling more bricks out of the wall. When he had made a biggish hole, he crept through it. Badger and the Smallest Fox followed him in.

They found themselves in a vast, damp, gloomy cellar. 'This is it!' cried Mr Fox.

'This is *what*?' said Badger. 'The place is empty.'

'Where are the turkeys?' asked the Smallest Fox, staring into the gloom. 'I thought Bean was a turkey man.'

'He is a turkey man,' said Mr Fox. 'But we're not after turkeys now. We've got plenty of food.'

'Then what *do* we need, Dad?'

'Take a good look round,' said Mr Fox. 'Don't you see *anything* that interests you?'

Badger and the Smallest Fox peered into the half-darkness. As their eyes became accustomed to the gloom, they began to see what looked like a whole lot of big glass jars standing upon shelves around the walls. They went closer. They *were* jars. There were hundreds of them, and upon each one was written the word CIDER.

The Smallest Fox leaped high in the air. 'Oh, Dad!' he cried out. 'Look what we've found! It's cider!'

'Ex-*actly*,' said Mr Fox.

'Tremendous!' shouted Badger.

'Bean's Secret Cider Cellar,' said Mr Fox. 'But go carefully, my dears. Don't make a noise. This cellar is right underneath the farmhouse itself.'

'Cider,' said Badger, 'is especially good for Badgers. We take it as medicine – one large glass three times a day with meals and another at bedtime.'

'It will make the feast into a banquet,' said Mr Fox.

While they were talking, the Smallest Fox had sneaked a jar off the shelf and had taken a gulp. 'Wow!' he gasped. 'Wow-*ee!*'

You must understand this was not the ordinary weak fizzy cider one buys in a store. It was the real stuff, a home-brewed fiery liquor that burned in your throat and boiled in your stomach.

'Ah-h-h-h-h-h!' gasped the Smallest Fox. 'This is *some* cider!'

'That's quite enough of that,' said Mr Fox, grabbing the jar and putting it to his own lips. He took a tremendous gulp. 'It's miraculous!' he whispered, fighting for breath. 'It's fabulous! It's beautiful!'

'It's my turn,' said Badger, taking the jar and tilting his head well back. The cider gurgled and bubbled down his throat. 'It's . . . it's like melted gold!' he gasped. 'Oh, Foxy, it's . . . like drinking sunbeams and rainbows!'

'You're poaching!' shrieked Rat. 'Put that down at once! There'll be none left for me!' Rat was perched upon the highest shelf in the cellar, peering out from behind a huge jar. There was a small rubber tube inserted in the neck of the jar, and Rat was using this tube to suck out the cider.

'You're drunk!' said Mr Fox.

'Mind your own business!' shrieked Rat. 'And if you great clumsy brutes come messing about in here we'll all be caught! Get out and leave me to sip my cider in peace.'

At that moment they heard a woman's voice calling out in the house above them. 'Hurry up and get that cider, Mabel!' the voice called. 'You know Mr Bean doesn't like to be kept waiting! Especially when he's been out all night in a tent!'

The animals froze. They stayed absolutely still, their ears pricked, their bodies tense. Then they heard the sound of a door being opened. The door was at the top of a flight of stone steps leading down from the house to the cellar.

And now someone was starting to come down those steps.

16   The Woman

'Quick!' said Mr Fox. 'Hide!' He and Badger and the Smallest Fox jumped up on to a shelf and crouched behind a row of big cider jars. Peering around the jars, they saw a huge woman coming down into the cellar. At the foot of the steps, the woman paused, looking to right and left. Then she turned and headed straight for the place where Mr Fox and Badger and the Smallest Fox were hiding. She stopped right in front of them. The only thing between her and them was a row of cider jars. She was so close, Mr Fox could hear the sound of her breathing. Peeping through the crack between two bottles, he noticed that she carried a big rolling-pin in one hand.

'How many will he want this time, Mrs Bean?' the woman shouted. And from the top of the steps the other voice called back, 'Bring up two or three jars.'

'He drank four yesterday, Mrs Bean.'

'Yes, but he won't want that many today because he's not going to be up there more than a few hours longer. He says the fox is bound to make a run for it this morning. It can't possibly stay down that hole another day without food.'

The woman in the cellar reached out and lifted a jar of cider from the shelf. The jar she took was next but one to the jar behind which Mr Fox was crouching.

'I'll be glad when the rotten brute is killed and strung up on the front porch,' she called out. 'And by the way, Mrs Bean, your husband promised I could have the tail as a souvenir.'

'The tail's been all shot to pieces,' said the voice from upstairs. 'Didn't you know that?'

'You mean it's *ruined*?'

'Of course it's ruined. They shot the tail but missed the fox.'

'Oh heck!' said the big woman. 'I did so want that tail!'

'You can have the head instead, Mabel. You can get it stuffed and hang it on your bedroom wall. Hurry up now with that cider!'

'Yes, Ma'am, I'm coming,' said the big woman, and she took a second jar from the shelf.

If she takes one more, she'll see us, thought Mr Fox. He could feel the Smallest Fox's body pressed tightly against his own, quivering with excitement.

'Will two be enough, Mrs Bean, or shall I take three?'

'My goodness, Mabel, I don't care so long as you get a move on!'

'Then two it is,' said the huge woman, speaking to herself now. 'He drinks too much anyway.'

Carrying a jar in each hand and with the rolling-pin tucked under one arm, she walked away across the cellar.

At the foot of the steps she paused and looked around, sniffing the air. 'There's rats down here again, Mrs Bean. I can smell 'em.'

'Then poison them, woman, poison them! You know where the poison's kept.'

'Yes, Ma'am,' Mabel said. She climbed slowly out of sight up the steps. The door slammed.

'Quick!' said Mr Fox. 'Grab a jar each and run for it!'

Rat stood on his high shelf and shrieked. 'What did I tell you! You nearly got nabbed, didn't you? You nearly gave the game away! You keep out of here from now on! I don't want you around! This is my place!'

'*You*,' said Mr Fox, 'are going to be poisoned.'

'Poppycock!' said Rat. 'I sit up here and watch her putting the stuff down. She'll never get *me*.'

Mr Fox and Badger and the Smallest Fox ran across the cellar clutching a gallon jar each. 'Goodbye, Rat!' they called out as they disappeared through the hole in the wall. 'Thanks for the lovely cider!'

'Thieves!' shrieked Rat. 'Robbers! Bandits! Burglars!'

The Great Feast

Back in the tunnel they paused so that Mr Fox could brick
up the hole in the wall. He was humming to himself as he
put the bricks back in place. 'I can still taste that glorious
cider,' he said. 'What an impudent fellow Rat is.'

'He has bad manners,' Badger said. 'All rats have bad
manners. I've never met a polite rat yet.'

'And he drinks too much,' said Mr Fox, putting the last
brick in place. 'There we are. Now, home to the feast!'

They grabbed their jars of cider and off they went. Mr
Fox was in front, the Smallest Fox came next and Badger
last. Along the tunnel they flew ... past the turning that
led to Bunce's Mighty Storehouse ... past Boggis's

Chicken House Number One and then up the long home stretch towards the place where they knew Mrs Fox would be waiting.

'Keep it up, my darlings!' shouted Mr Fox. 'We'll soon be there! Think what's waiting for us at the other end! And just think what we're bringing home with us in these jars! That ought to cheer up poor Mrs Fox.' Mr Fox sang a little song as he ran:

> 'Home again swiftly I glide,
> Back to my beautiful bride.
> She'll not feel so rotten
> As soon as she's gotten
> Some cider inside her inside.'

Then Badger joined in:

> 'Oh poor Mrs Badger, he cried,
> So hungry she very near died.
> But she'll not feel so hollow
> If only she'll swallow
> Some cider inside her inside.'

They were still singing as they rounded the final corner and burst in upon the most wonderful and amazing sight any of them had ever seen. The feast was just beginning. A large dining-room had been hollowed out of the earth, and in the middle of it, seated around a huge table, were no less than twenty-nine animals. They were:

Mrs Fox and three Small Foxes.

Mrs Badger and three Small Badgers.

Mole and Mrs Mole and four Small Moles.

Rabbit and Mrs Rabbit and five Small Rabbits.

Weasel and Mrs Weasel and six Small Weasels.

The table was covered with chickens and ducks and geese and hams and bacon, and everyone was tucking into the lovely food.

'My darling!' cried Mrs Fox, jumping up and hugging Mr Fox. 'We couldn't wait! Please forgive us!' Then she hugged the Smallest Fox of all, and Mrs Badger hugged Badger, and everyone hugged everyone else. Amid shouts of joy, the great jars of cider were placed upon the table, and Mr Fox and Badger and the Smallest Fox sat down with the others.

You must remember no one had eaten a thing for several days. They were ravenous. So for a while there was no conversation at all. There was only the sound of crunching and chewing as the animals attacked the succulent food.

At last, Badger stood up. He raised his glass of cider and called out, 'A toast! I want you all to stand and drink a toast to our dear friend who has saved our lives this day – Mr Fox!'

'To Mr Fox!' they all shouted, standing up and raising their glasses. 'To Mr Fox! Long may he live!'

428

Then Mrs Fox got shyly to her feet and said, 'I don't want to make a speech. I just want to say one thing, and it is this: MY HUSBAND IS A FANTASTIC FOX.' Everyone clapped and cheered. Then Mr Fox himself stood up.

'This delicious meal . . .' he began, then he stopped. In the silence that followed, he let fly a tremendous belch. There was laughter and more clapping. 'This delicious meal, my friends,' he went on, 'is by courtesy of Messrs Boggis, Bunce and Bean.' (More cheering and laughter.) 'And I hope you have enjoyed it as much as I have.' He let fly another colossal belch.

'Better out than in,' said Badger.

'Thank you,' said Mr Fox, grinning hugely. 'But now, my friends, let us be serious. Let us think of tomorrow and the next day and the days after that. If we go out, we will be killed. Right?'

'Right!' they shouted.

'We'll be shot before we've gone a yard,' said Badger.

'Ex-*actly*,' said Mr Fox. 'But who *wants* to go out, anyway; let me ask you that? We are all diggers, every one of us. We hate the outside. The outside is full of enemies. We only go out because we have to, to get food for our families. But now, my friends, we have an entirely new set-up. We have a safe tunnel leading to three of the finest stores in the world!'

'We do indeed!' said Badger. 'I've seen 'em!'

'And you know what this means?' said Mr Fox. '*It means that none of us need ever go out into the open again!*'

There was a buzz of excitement around the table.

'I therefore invite you all,' Mr Fox went on, 'to stay here with me for ever.'

'For ever!' they cried. 'My goodness! How marvellous!' And Rabbit said to Mrs Rabbit, 'My dear, just think! We're never going to be shot at again in our lives!'

'We will make,' said Mr Fox, 'a little underground village, with streets and houses on each side – separate houses for Badgers and Moles and Rabbits and Weasels and Foxes. And every day I will go shopping for you all. And every day we will eat like kings.'

The cheering that followed this speech went on for many minutes.

Still Waiting

Outside the fox's hole, Boggis and Bunce and Bean sat beside their tents with their guns on their laps. It was beginning to rain. Water was trickling down the necks of the three men and into their shoes.

'He won't stay down there much longer now,' Boggis said.

'The brute must be famished,' Bunce said.

'That's right,' Bean said. 'He'll be making a dash for it any moment. Keep your guns handy.'

They sat there by the hole, waiting for the fox to come out.

And so far as I know, they are still waiting.

The BFG

by Roald Dahl

Gloriumptious ... Jumbly ... Hopscotchy

The BFG uses some extraordinary words, but then he's no ordinary giant. He's the kindest giant you could hope to meet and he turns out to be Sophie's best friend. The trouble is, not all giants are quite as friendly, and Sophie and the BFG set out to rid the world of the Bloodbottler, the Fleshlumpeater, the Bonecruncher and other nasty giants for ever.

Charlie and the Great Glass Elevator

by Roald Dahl

'You see this green button. I must press it at exactly the right instant.'

Mr Wonka might be a genius with chocolate, but Charlie and his family don't trust his flying skills one bit. Especially when the thing he's flying is a glass elevator and it's zooming out of control into the stratosphere. But life is never dull with Mr Wonka and if he gets them into some terrible scrapes, he's sure to be able to get them out ... isn't he?

Danny the Champion of the World

by Roald Dahl

'I am going to let you in on the deepest, darkest secret of my whole life.'

Danny thinks the world of his father, but imagine his surprise when he finds out he's been breaking the law! Even grown-ups bend the rules sometimes, but Danny knows his father is still good, kind and clever and full of exciting ideas.

Join them in this thrilling adventure as they hope to pull off the most daring and dangerous plan ever.

George's Marvellous Medicine

by Roald Dahl

'You're growing too fast. Boys who grow too fast become stupid and lazy.'

George's grandma has some pretty odd views. In fact, she's not a very nice person at all. She thinks caterpillars and slugs are delicious and likes to crunch on beetles best of all. George can do nothing right in Grandma's eyes, so when it's time for her medicine he decides to give her a dose of his own special brew.

Matilda

by Roald Dahl

Cheat ... Stupid ... Ignorant ... Liar

Matilda's parents have called her some terrible things. The truth is, she's a genius and they're the stupid ones. Find out how she gets the better of them and her spiteful headmistress, Miss Trunchbull, as well as discovering that she has a very special power.

The Witches

by Roald Dahl

Witches think children smell of dogs' droppings!
The Grand High Witch and her wicked followers
hate children so much that they plan to get rid of
every child in England. Luckily the boy in this
story uncovers the plot and his grandmother is a
witch expert, but witches are extremely dangerous
and not everything goes quite to plan.

Winner of the Whitbread Award

The Roald Dahl Foundation

Registered Charity
No. 1004230

Throughout his life Roald Dahl gave of his time and money to help people in need. When he died, his widow, Felicity Dahl, established The Roald Dahl Foundation to continue this generous tradition. The Foundation's aim is to serve people in the UK in three major areas:

- **Literacy**, because it was Roald's crusade. Literacy is the most basic educational tool. It is also the passport to hours of pleasure. For many reasons, some people and some groups need extra assistance to help them achieve this essential skill. The Foundation offers grants to a diverse group in this area.

- **Neurology**, because brain damage has severely affected the Dahl family. Neurology funds specialize in the areas of epilepsy and head injury. In addition to our ongoing programme of individual grants to people in financial hardship, the Foundation grants funds to specially identified projects.

- **Haematology**, because leukaemia was the cause of Roald's death. Our haematology grants target areas where funds are particularly hard to come by, but where the need is undeniably great. In addition to many individual grants, the Foundation supports large scale projects.

All monies donated to the Foundation are directed where they are required – to people in the UK with specific needs. If you would like to know more about us, or help the Foundation in its work by making a donation, then please write to us direct:

**The Roald Dahl Foundation
92 High Street
Great Missenden
Buckinghamshire HP16 0AN
England**

READ MORE IN PUFFIN

For children of all ages, Puffin represents quality and variety – the very best in publishing today around the world.

For complete information about books available from Puffin – and Penguin – and how to order them, contact us at the appropriate address below. Please note that for copyright reasons the selection of books varies from country to country.

On the World Wide Web: www.penguin.co.uk

In the United Kingdom: Please write to *Dept. EP, Penguin Books Ltd, Bath Road, Harmondsworth, West Drayton, Middlesex UB7 ODA*

In the United States: Please write to *Penguin Putnam inc., P.O. Box 12289, Dept B, Newark, New Jersey 07101-5289* or call 1-800-788-6262.

In Canada: Please write to *Penguin Books Canada Ltd, 10 Alcorn Avenue, Suite 300, Toronto, Ontario M4V 3B2*

In Australia: Please write to *Penguin Books Australia Ltd, P.O. Box 257, Ringwood, Victoria 3134*

In New Zealand: Please write to *Penguin Books (NZ) Ltd, Private Bag 102902, North Shore Mail Centre, Auckland 10*

In India: Please write to *Penguin Books India Pvt Ltd, 11 Panscheel Shopping Centre, Panscheel Park, New Delhi 110 017*

In the Netherlands: Please write to *Penguin Books Netherlands bv, Postbus 3507, NL-1001 AH Amsterdam*

In Germany: Please write to *Penguin Books Deutschland GmbH, Metzlerstrasse 26, 60594 Frankfurt am Main*

In Spain: Please write to *Penguin Books S. A., Bravo Murillo 19, 1° B, 28015 Madrid*

In Italy: Please write to *Penguin Italia s.r.l., Via Felice Casati 20, I–20124 Milano*

In France: Please write to *Penguin France S. A., 17 rue Lejeune, F–31000 Toulouse*

In Japan: Please write to *Penguin Books Japan, Ishikiribashi Building, 2-5-4, Suido, Bunkyo-ku, Tokyo 112*

In South Africa: Please write to *Longman Penguin Southern Africa (Pty) Ltd, Private Bag X08, Bertsham 2013*